Critical Guides to French Texts

53 La Chastelaine de Vergi *and*
   Jean Renart: Le Lai de l'ombre

Critical Guides to French Texts

EDITED BY ROGER LITTLE, WOLFGANG VAN EMDEN, DAVID WILLIAMS

La Chastelaine de Vergi

and

Jean Renart:
Le Lai de l'ombre

Paula Clifford

Lecturer in French,
University of Reading

Grant & Cutler Ltd
1986

© Grant & Cutler Ltd
1986
ISBN 0 7293 0235 0

I.S.B.N. 84-599-1111-X

DEPÓSITO LEGAL: V. 2.031 - 1985

Printed in Spain by
Artes Gráficas Soler, S.A., Valencia
for
GRANT & CUTLER LTD
11 BUCKINGHAM STREET, LONDON W.C.2

Contents

Pains of love be sweeter far
Than all other pleasures are.

(Dryden)

Preface

The following editions have been used for this study:

La Chastelaine de Vergi edited by F. Whitehead, Manchester University Press, 2nd edition, 1951, last reprinted in 1982.

Le Lay de l'ombre edited by B.J. Levy and A. Hindley, Hull French Texts, 1977.

The edition of *Le Lai de l'ombre* by John Orr, published by Edinburgh University Press (1948) is now out of print but is also recommended if obtainable. This book had already gone to press when the collection of texts edited by René Stuip appeared under the general title of *La Châtelaine de Vergy* (Paris, 10/18, Série "Bibliothèque Médiévale", 1985). This contains the medieval text (based on BN f.fr. 375), together with a translation, an all too brief introduction and a few textual notes. It is followed by three 15th- and 16th-century adaptations of the original. References to the bibliography at the end of this volume are in the form of an italicized number, followed by a page reference where appropriate.

I should like to thank Professor Wolfgang van Emden and Professor Roger Little for their detailed and helpful comments on the manuscript of this book. I am also grateful to my fellow medievalists in the University of Reading for offering a particularly congenial and stimulating environment in which to work.

Paula Clifford
Reading, 1984.

Preface

Paul Churchland
Berlin, 1984.

Introduction

When two literary works are brought together initially for critical convenience it is tempting to look for similarities or shared features, either real or imagined, to justify (consciously or otherwise) their inclusion in the same volume. Most of this book will be devoted to independent discussions of *La Chastelaine de Vergi* and *Le Lai de l'ombre*, and only the first and last sections will be concerned with their relation to each other and to thirteenth-century French literature in general. Nevertheless, as I have studied these two texts for the purpose of writing this book, I have frequently found myself comparing and contrasting them, and it seems useful to draw attention to these points of contact before embarking on the separate analyses.

The form of these two poems (which are, coincidentally, of almost equal length) has not aroused very much critical comment. Bibliographers tend to group them under the heading of *lai* rather than romance, but neither description is particularly satisfactory. Although there are certain similarities with the twelfth-century *lai* as exemplified by the compositions of Marie de France (see further p.12 below), both *La Chastelaine de Vergi* and *Le Lai de l'ombre* reflect the evolution in the genre by the thirteenth century. As several literary historians have pointed out, this was a time for consolidating twelfth-century forms and traditions rather than for creating new ones (see, for example, *8* and *9*). In particular, all reference to a musical origin or connection for the *lai* has been dropped, along with any appeal to oral tradition, and the narrative is all-important. It is not hard to see in these works an early form of the *nouvelle* or short story, whether this may consist of a succession of events (as in *La Chastelaine de Vergi*) or of a single encounter between two people (*Le Lai de l'ombre*). In addition both are, of course, love stories, whose protagonists are unnamed, and both illustrate a certain moral. On the negative side, *La Chastelaine de Vergi* demonstrates the dangers of indiscretion, while *Le Lai de l'ombre* offers a positive example of the important combination of *Amors* and *sens*.

The literary background of these compositions is the twelfth-century convention of courtly love. Much has been written on this, and the subject need not detain us long here. It is well known that the early thirteenth century saw the collapse of the social structure of the great feudal courts in southern France, where the courtly lyric had originated some 120-130 years earlier, and that by the time of the Albigensian crusades (1209-29) the Provençal literary movement seemed in any case to be drawing to a natural close. There were two developments possible. The first was a highly formalized genre concerned more with the theory and ideals of courtly love than with their application. This was the direction taken by the mainstream of the Provençal lyric and some echoes of it may be found in *Le Lai de l'ombre*. The second possibility was the more complete transition to a narrative form — the ideals of courtly love being demonstrated and worked out in reality — and this is the approach pioneered by Marie de France and Chrétien de Troyes and reflected in *La Chastelaine de Vergi*. In both poems we shall see many elements drawn from the courtly love tradition, which the two authors have arranged and adapted in their own fashion, in line with much thirteenth-century writing. However, two features which are common to both texts seem to be particularly typical of the courtly tradition: the importance accorded to discretion, on the part both of the characters and of the author himself, and the irony which appears to be inherent in the courtly narrative.

It could be that the two texts are roughly contemporaneous, although attempts to date them have produced quite divergent claims. The most plausible effort is the dating of *Le Lai de l'ombre* between 1219 and 1222, which is based on the identi-fication of the 'Eslit' (l.41) as Miles de Nanteuil, Bishop-elect of Beauvais at that time (see *31* and *27*, p.246ff.), although earlier suggestions had placed the work as late as the middle of the century. A similar shift in opinion can be seen in the dating of

La Chastelaine de Vergi. Some recent criticism has placed it in
the first 30 or 40 years of the thirteenth century, though perhaps
not earlier than 1228, the date of Renart's *Guillaume de Dôle*, in
which the author boasts of being the first to quote lyric poetry in
a *roman*, a technique also used in *La Chastelaine de Vergi* (see
25, pp.63-65). On the other hand, Zumthor has also argued for a
date at the end of the century, and there seems to be little
evidence for either point of view.

As far as the author and his language are concerned, the
picture is again much clearer in the case of *Le Lai de l'ombre*.
Nothing at all is known of the author of *La Chastelaine de Vergi*
and linguistic studies of the text have not allowed any definite
conclusions to be reached as to its region of origin. The author
of *Le Lai de l'ombre*, however, names himself (l.953) and some
light is thrown on the text by studies of other works attributed to
Jean Renart (see in particular R. Lejeune-Dehousse's compre-
hensive study *(27)*).

The dates and authorship of the two compositions are nonetheless relatively minor details. The most important thing is that
we have here two good examples of the development of the love
'adventure' in verse form in the thirteenth century. Freed from
the unrealistic idealism of the courtly lyric and from the complexities of plot of some of the longer courtly *romans*, these two
works both have an interest that transcends the literary confines
of their day. Each, in different measure, illustrates Stevens's
assertion that 'In the greater medieval love-romances are present
all the principal motifs which characterize the experience of
romantic love in subsequent ages' (*7*, p.34).

1. *La Chastelaine de Vergi:* The Structure of the Poem

(i) *A tri-partite* lai *structure*

The appearance of *La Chastelaine de Vergi* is closely allied to that of the *lai* as it was established by Marie de France, writing around 1170, and imitated by a number of other writers in the twelfth and thirteenth centuries. Originally a purely musical composition, the term *lai* was used by Marie to refer also to the story which was set to that music. By the thirteenth century it was being used quite unambiguously of the short narrative composition itself, and the musical connotation (which remains in English) had been lost. The average length of a *lai* has been put at around 500 lines (see Dubuis, *2*, ch.2), although some were much shorter, for example Marie de France's *Chèvrefoil* (118 lines) or the anonymous *Lay de Doon* (286 lines). In this respect *La Chastelaine de Vergi* resembles the two longer *lais* of Marie de France — *Eliduc* (1184 lines) and *Guigemar* (886 lines) — both of which have a longer train of events to be presented. The verse form is a straightforward one — rhyming octosyllabics — and the action is framed by a prologue and an epilogue. These two small sections, which were little more than routine niceties in Marie de France, have a much greater significance in *La Chastelaine de Vergi*, for they set out the meaning the reader is to draw from the tale.

The content of the twelfth-century *lai* could be defined fairly closely. Set in the distant past (sometimes but not always in Celtic lands), the stories are adventures of love, which draw on the terminology of courtly literature. The main characters tend to be aristocrats who move in the noble circles which produced the literary conceit of courtliness. The action often includes some supernatural being, event or allusion. However, this latter feature, which was in any case sometimes attenuated in Marie's writing in the interests of realism, disappears completely in the thirteenth-century form. Thus while some of the events in *La Chastelaine de Vergi* may strike the modern reader as somewhat improbable, a concern for realism is shown, for instance, in the choice of genuine Burgundian names. We shall see later that some critics have seen close parallels between *La Chastelaine de Vergi* and particular *lais*, especially Marie de France's *Lanval* and the anonymous *Guingamor*. The similarity is primarily a thematic one, but there is also a formal likeness which should not be disregarded.

Critics who have considered the internal structure of *La Chastelaine de Vergi* have differed considerably in their interpretations, which have been based variously on thematic, linguistic and structuralist criteria. Zumthor (*20*, p.242) has argued that there are two thematic 'lines' in the poem, one being based on the concept of *fine amors* and the other deriving from the tradition of the *fabliau*. These strains he sees as coming together in the figure of the knight, who has a role in both series of events — as lover and as the duke's vassal. This duality of themes leads him to posit a binary structure. A dual structure is also implied by Payen's analysis (*15*) which distinguishes the forms of tragedy and of the *exemplum*. The tragic events are set between two episodes (the lovers' meeting and the heroine's monologue) in which the author sets out the meaning of the tragedy.

Two other critics have based their analyses on the similarity with *Lanval*. Maraud (*14*) establishes a parallel, although more complex, structure for *La Chastelaine de Vergi* based on a number of narrative elements which the poems seem to have in common. He suggests a threefold structure comprising the three very general motifs of the temptress, the betrayed secret, and proof of innocence. Arrathoon (*10*) interprets both poems in terms of folklore structures (a subject which first became popular in the 1960s, following the translation of studies by the Russian formalist writers of the 1930s). She concludes that the two poems are closely related structurally, although there is little superficial resemblance between them, thereby revealing a rather sweeping disregard for points of detail.

La Chastelaine de Vergi is set firmly in the tradition of the *lai* by Dubuis, who sees it as a transitional work between *lai* and *nouvelle*, and who also imposes on it a linear structure (*2*, p.523), perhaps to bring it into line with the earlier form. Shirt, on the other hand, arguing on the basis of linguistic and stylistic features, sees a circular shape and concludes: 'The romance world within the circle is ... mimetically self-contained and morally autonomous — in short not unlike that of the lyric poet' (*18*, p.86). It is this idea of a circle which I should like to take up now, but to associate it with a tripartite structure which is characteristic of many *lais*, although, as Dubuis rightly suggests, these do tend to be more linear in form.

As I see it, the structure of *La Chastelaine de Vergi* hinges on the narrative treatment of the theme of disclosure or revelation which dominates the work. There are three major episodes in which the lovers' secret is disclosed, and the text falls neatly into three sections, each having roughly 300 lines, and each containing one such episode, although this may not constitute the main event in that section. Thus part one, where the main event is that of the temptress rebuffed, culminates in the knight's disclosure of his affair to the duke (ll.340-58). Part two, concerned mainly with the knight demonstrating his innocence to the duke, culminates in the duke's disclosure to his wife (ll.647-58). In part three the order is reversed: it begins with a disclosure — the duchess reveals her knowledge of events to the chastelaine (ll.707-18) — which precipitates the final tragedy.

This tripartite division of the text echoes the structure of various *lais*, but it is oversimplified in that it does not take account of the prologue and epilogue, which are of crucial importance. The prologue, after a general beginning (ll.1-17), also takes the form of a disclosure, that by the author to his audience, as he summarizes the details of the affair between two lovers yet to be introduced. This revelation is important, for it is from the reader's awareness of events that the irony in the narrative emerges. In other words, the stylistic device of irony which characterizes so much of the work springs from an initial disclosure, just as the tragic note which dominates the end of the story emanates in particular from the disclosure by the duchess — hence the reversed order of events in part three. The story is in a sense open-ended, for the duke is the only character left alive, and this allows for the realistic, although unstated, possibility of the details of the narrative being transmitted further, thus bringing us back to the beginning again.

The 'circle' of disclosure begins at a point which is not recounted in *La Chastelaine de Vergi*, where the chastelaine granted her love to the knight. This is the secret which, for reasons unstated, must not be divulged. It may be, as Kostoroski suggests, that secrecy is for the chastelaine 'the symbol of the most perfect fidelity' (*12*, p.182) and the story thus becomes one of ever greater betrayal. The secret is disclosed by the knight to the duke, by the duke to the duchess, and by the duchess back to the chastelaine herself. At this point the circle is retraced in a succession of tragedies. Once the secret is known to, and passed on by, all the protagonists, it is then revealed to society at large through the events involving the death of three of the four characters. The chastelaine's suicide provokes that of her lover, which in turn involves the duke in the tragic act of killing his wife. The duke, however, remains alive to transmit the story more widely than just to those witnessing the actual events. Once the circle of disclosure has been completed, then, concern for secrecy and the ironic overtones are replaced by the theme and language of tragedy.

These two themes are united only in the prologue and epilogue. Interestingly, the note of tragedy is more apparent in the prologue, immediately before the theme of concealing love is introduced, while the epilogue reiterates the importance of secrecy, once the tragic end to the story has been recounted. Thus after the first eight lines of the prologue with its opposition between *conseil celer* (1.3) and *descuevre* (1.5) the dominant note, if not tragic, is increasingly one of sorrow; 'cil joie en pert' (1.9) leads to 'tant com l'amor est plus grant / sont plus mari li fin amant' (ll.11-12) and culminates in

> et sovent tel meschief en vient
> que l'amor faillir en covient
> a grant dolor et a vergoingne
> si comme il avint en Borgoingne ...
>
> (ll.15-18)

In the epilogue, however (ll.944-58), the exclamation of dismay in line 944 leads back to the idea 'celer devoit' (l.947) with the moral:

> Et par cest example doit l'en
> s'amor celer par si grant sen
>   (ll.951-52)

The two themes, as well as the formal beginning and end of the poem, are also linked through the traditional figures who constitute a threat to the *fin amant*. In the prologue they are described rather than named — they pretend to be loyal (l.2) but derive amusement from revealing secrets (ll.8-9). The concluding lines of the poem return to them using stronger language: they are the 'faus felons enquereors / qui enquierent autrui amors' (ll.957-58). It must be pointed out, however, that the tragedy is not to be laid at the door of slanderers. In this respect, as Payen points out (*15*, p.209), there is a certain *décalage* between the content of the prologue and the real meaning of the work. Instead the emphasis remains very much on the duty of lovers to keep their secret, for 'li descouvrirs riens n'avance' (l.954), and the story itself shows that 'those who pry' are not to be identified with mere character types (the familiar *losengiers*). The secret is disclosed by both the knight and the duke, not without due thought for the consequences, to those to whom they are bound in either feudal or marital trust.

Thus the meaning of 'disclosure' is amplified in the course of *La Chastelaine de Vergi*, and I should like now to consider its treatment and with it the gradual turning of the circle, through each of the three parts of the poem. It must be said, however, that this is purely a convenient thematic division. The form of the text is that of a continuous whole (which perhaps reinforces the impression of a circular structure) and unlike most *lais* does not offer clear breaks, marked by short descriptive or recapitulatory passages. The movement of the narrative thus appears inexorable; no sooner is the culminating point of one episode reached than we are plunged immediately into the development of the next. As Payen observes: 'Dès le début de l'œuvre apparaît la phrase longue, enchaînant sans rupture des moments successifs, qui caractérise le style de la *Châtelaine* et contribue à son unité' (*15*, p.211).

(ii) *From disclosure to tragedy: analysis of the poem*

a) *Introduction (ll.1-42) and part one (ll.43-358)*

There is one further point to be made on the prologue to the poem. The traditional courtly love lyric frequently introduces the *losengiers* (the Provençal term for 'slanderers') as a vague threat, and nearly always insists on the need for secrecy. Less often mentioned, however, are the consequences for the lovers if their secret is revealed; nor do we know the identity or behaviour of these slanderers. In contrast, at the beginning of *La Chastelaine de Vergi* we are given a very precise indication of the danger to the lovers: each thinks the other has betrayed them (ll.13-14). This is obviously not quite the moral of the story that follows, for it is only the lady who assumes infidelity (both verbal and sexual) on the part of her lover, but it is a general conclusion that may be drawn. Similarly, we are told that the greater the love the greater the anguish of the *fin amant* (ll.11-12), and this in fact understates the lesson of a love story which ends in death.

After the general prologue, lines 19 to 42 may be seen as an introduction to the main events of the poem, a pattern which again follows that typical of the longer *lai*. It may be noted here that the author's technique is to disguise this structural break by linking the last line of the prologue (l.17) with the first line of the introduction (l.18) in a rhyming couplet (cf. the reverse procedure at the end of the poem, in lines 943-44). In this introduction, which translates the general precepts of the prologue into a particular situation, the emphasis is on secrecy — which is seen particularly, in concrete terms, in the description of the way in which the lovers meet — but this also combines a hint of tragedy in lines 21-28.

Line 23 introduces the *couvenant* made by the lady, which is a promise of her love with the stipulation of secrecy. If the covenant is broken her love will be lost (l.26) — a condition reminiscent of that laid down by the fairy in *Lanval*:

> 'A tuz jurs m'avriez perdue,
> Se ceste amur esteit seüe...'
>
> (*Lanval*, ll.147-48)

The secrecy theme itself is perhaps enhanced by the fact that the knight is not named, and the other characters are known only by their titles. It is significant from the point of view of the poem's structure that the reason for secrecy is not made explicit. Most critics assume that we are dealing with the situation typical of courtly romance and that the heroine is married (see Reed's article (*16*) on this), although the only textual justification for this assumption is the chastelaine's reference in line 714 to *mon seignor* (who might arguably be her uncle the duke). But the important structural consequence of this omission lies in the absence of a husband, who would otherwise need to be the main character to whom any disclosure might be made; the presence of such a figure would detract from the tight structure of the poem outlined above. Similarly, the absence of any human go-between or confidant, which is implied by the detail of the dog in lines 34ff., and which provokes the surprise of the duke in line 346, keeps events in the control of the four protagonists.

In the main part of the first section (ll.43-358) the pattern is maintained of a dominant theme of secrecy, together with a *leit-motif* of tragedy, which is inherent in the idea of breaking the promise of secrecy. It is the hidden nature of the knight's love that leaves him vulnerable to the approaches of the duchess, and he is forced into revelation to safeguard his relationship with his overlord as well as with his lady (insofar as the 'punishment' of exile is averted). The developing situation has various ironic features, while the tragic motif is contained in the potentially tragic figure of the knight, as the following examples show.

There is irony to be found here in the interaction of the duchess and the knight, and of the duchess and her husband. The former interaction is seen in lines 49-58, in the *semblant* of the knight. The author tells us that the knight would have realized the duchess's intentions — and, by implication, have been able to save himself — 's'il n'eüst le cuer aillors' (l.50). But, ironically, it is the knight's apparent lack of a mistress which is a weapon in the hands of the duchess (ll.136-37). Ironically again, the duchess unwittingly suggests a means of escape for the knight, which her husband takes up in lines 261-64: proof of a mistress would exonerate him. Secret love, then, firstly exposes the knight to the attention of the duchess, and secondly offers an opportunity for combatting her advances.

The tragic element in this part lies particularly in the anguish of the knight, who is caught in the dilemma as to whether to obey his feudal oath of allegiance to the duke or to honour his promise to the chastelaine, and thus Lakits (*13*, p.73) is led to see him as an inherently tragic figure. This view is borne out by lines 177-89, which portray the knight's anguish on the immediate realization that whichever solution he chooses he will lose his mistress, and culminate in the words:

> si est en si grant desconfort
> qu'a mort se tient et a trahi
> (ll.188-89)

The reference to death is prepared by the expressions of extreme anguish (*ire, mautalent* (l.178), *tramblant* (l.179)) and the conventional expression of uncourtliness (*trahitor desloial* (l.186)). It is interesting that the possibility of exile, necessitating geographical distance from his mistress, is mentioned first, perhaps as the more obvious form of loss, and is reminiscent of the courtly convention of *amor de lonh*. The unreasoned fear of losing the lady through betraying their secret, albeit in thoroughly extenuating circumstances, comes second. It is only later, when the depth of the chastelaine's love is revealed in her monologue, that we realize the full significance and likelihood of this alternative. It is therefore ironic that the knight agrees with alacrity to swear to answer the duke truthfully (ll.218-24) as a means of avoiding his dilemma ('cele perte / comme de guerpir la contree / ou cele est qui plus li agree', ll.228-30), since this will lead inexorably to his downfall. It seems that the author is

hinting at the same lack of attention on the part of the knight as
we have already seen in his dealings with the duchess:

> ... qu'il ne pensse ne ne regarde
> de ce dont li duc se prent garde
> (ll.233-34)

and this begins to add up to a potentially tragic singlemindedness.

The duke's reply (ll.241-67) makes it quite clear that the
knight has unwittingly agreed to reveal the secret, the question
being centred on whether or not he loves elsewhere (ll.261-64).
There is an accompanying touch of irony in the duke's remark
that if he refuses 'comme parjurs vous en alez' (l.266), since the
knight will otherwise be *parjurs* with respect to the chastelaine,
and this point is made in the resumed account of the knight's
dilemma (ll.268-302). It seems that the knight is under no
illusions as to what will happen if he breaks his promise, and
again the consequence is expressed in the phrase 'a mort se tient'
(l.273), which is fairly conventional in the courtly lyric, but in
this context assumes tragic overtones. The result of these
deliberations is a visible distress, and the four lines portraying
this (ll.308-11) increase the impression of a tragic figure.
However, this is relegated to a background detail as our interest
is concentrated both on the disclosure that is about to take place
and also on the possibility of further disclosure, which the duke,
in a grave and lengthy oath (ll.332-39), swears he will not permit.
In contrast to this long exchange between the duke and his vassal
the knight's actual revelation is made in just two lines:

> 'j'aim vostre niece de Vergi,
> et ele moi, tant c'om puet plus'
> (ll.343-44)

and the details of their meetings are conveyed in the four lines of
narrative which conclude part one of the poem.

b) *Part two (ll.359-667)*

Following the revealing of the secret to the duke at the end of part one, it is the motif of disclosure rather than secrecy that comes to dominate part two, although the former theme is contained in many allusions to concealment and appearances. Irony is correspondingly less marked, but there are more and more tragic overtones in this section as the story progresses. The verbal disclosure of the previous section is followed by its demonstrated proof. Although it may seem a greater invasion of privacy to have the duke witness the lovers' meeting rather than simply be told about it, the knight has no hesitation in granting this request. His reply even involves some lighthearted play on words, on the homonymic *annuit* (*ennuie* and *à nuit*: ll.367-68, 370, 374). The fact of betrayal is contained in the emphasis laid on the identity of the knight's mistress as the duke's niece, for she is thus referred to wherever possible (ll.365, 376, 380, 422). With this identity established and the secret relationship fully revealed to the duke, there is considerable irony in the duke's pleasure at the knight's innocence with respect to his wife (l.427), for this knowledge will bring about the lovers' tragedy. Indeed this happens very quickly because the duke is unable to engage in any kind of dissimulation himself; on their return he displays excessive warmth towards the knight:

> ... monstra li dus au chevalier
> plus biau samblant qu'ainz n'avoit fait
> (ll.510-11)

There is, however, a certain weakness in the narrative here, inevitable, perhaps, because of the requirements of the story, in that the duke appears unmoved by his wife's treachery and takes no recriminating action against her.

The touching scene of the lovers' meeting has little bearing on the thematic lines that we are following, except insofar as it illustrates the suffering inherent in a concealed love relationship. The detail of the lovers arranging their next meeting (ll.470-71) shows us that their relationship is able to survive the secret being shared, until it is actually disclosed to the chastelaine herself (unlike the affair in *Lanval* which is terminated at once). After their parting, however, the theme of secrecy returns immediately, as the knight eloquently begs the duke to 'cest conseil celer' (l.499) and adds a warning as to the consequences if he does not:

> '... amor perdroie et joie et aise
> et morroie sanz nule faute'
>   (ll.500-01)

Again we see that the courtly convention of loss of love entailing the metaphorical death of the lover is, in retrospect, to be interpreted literally in *La Chastelaine de Vergi*. The duke's promise is quickly made:

> 'sachiez qu'il ert si bien celé
> que ja par moi n'en ert parlé'
>   (ll.505-06)

and *bien celé* is again ironic in view of the speed with which the secret seems to be passed on.

The second part moves towards its climax with the portrayal of the persistence of the duchess in trying to get the duke to reveal the secret. In contrast to the behaviour of her guileless husband the duchess's words and actions are characterized by dissimulation, with the word *samblant* recurring several times. She begins with an ambiguous speech (ll.577-86) which completely hides its true intention. She sees her husband's oath of secrecy as an expression of distrust in her (ll.622-23) and the duke acknowledges the force of this argument:

> '... tant m'afi en vous et croi
> que chose celer ne vous doi'
>   (ll.637-38)

Once again, as the secret is revealed, allusions to death return. It seems a little unlikely that such a loving husband should threaten his wife with certain death if she betrays a confidence (l.643), but this is nonetheless accepted and even amplified by the duchess herself: 'que il la pende a une hart' (l.667). Significantly, her reaction to the unwelcome confidence is to conceal her true emotion — 'ainc de ce samblant ne fist' (l.663) — promising instead to 'celer ceste oevre' (l.665). Thus the second part of the poem closes with this further revelation and with overtones of death having been associated with all four characters. As disclosure has taken over from secrecy, so the tragic tone gradually replaces the ironic one.

c) *Part three (ll.668-958)*

In the final part of *La Chastelaine de Vergi* the pattern of the first two sections is reversed. From line 668 onwards we see the duchess impatient to reveal the secret entrusted to her, and the remainder of the story is concerned with the tragic consequences of her action. There seems to be a progression in the speed with which the three characters are prepared to share the lovers' secret: the knight's revelation is delayed by his monologue, while the duke capitulates in the course of conversation. The duchess shows no hesitation at all and her intention is quite clear from the outset — 'ne ja ne celera tel chose' (l.679) — a detail which is sufficient to rank her with the uncourtly ladies and slanderers of tradition. The ethic of love represented by the chastelaine and her knight finds its negation in the figure of the duchess, before the events which she instigates actually destroy the lovers themselves.

At lines 681-82 we have the only reference to passing time in the whole work, and this underlines the strength of the feelings which continue to characterize the duchess. She still appears above all as one who hides her feelings — 'son corage celer set' (l.692) — and she is still impatient to break her promise to her husband (l.697). It may perhaps be seen as ironic that while *celer* is a virtue when it refers to the discretion of lovers, *celer* in the sense of dissimulation is, in *La Chastelaine de Vergi*, a characteristic of the person who causes the downfall of a pair who have practised discretion as far as was possible in their social context.

We then witness the effects of this revelation on the
chastelaine (ll.723ff.), and from this point, as tragedy becomes
the dominant theme, she appears as a tragic heroine. There
continue to be some touches of irony, as, for example, where the
reader knows the chastelaine's assumption of her lover's
infidelity with the duchess to be unfounded, and, indeed, to be
the reverse of the true situation. The lady's lament alludes in
passing to the tragic lovers Tristan and Iseut (l.760) and
fleetingly recalls the theme of *descouvrir* (l.771) before
becoming a more general confession of tragic love (ll.772ff.).
The idea of death in a non-metaphorical sense is made explicit
(ll.803, 805, 815) although this refers at first to the heroine's
desire to die if her lover should die before her. Lines 808-14
return to the broken promise, and combine the themes of the
secret (l.812), the loss of the lady (l.813) and disclosure (l.814).
Although the same question as to why the need for secrecy at all
may be at the back of one's mind at lines 809-10, the dominant
note is now wholly tragic; even so, the actual death of the
heroine comes as a shock. The author seems to recognize this,
for lines 835-40 could equally well denote fainting (cf. the
confusion between death and a coma in Marie de France's
Eliduc). The ambiguity is resolved only when the knight admits
that she is indeed dead (ll.870, 872). Lines 840ff. offer an ironic
contrast between the chastelaine's tragic end and the scene of the
dancing downstairs, where no-one is aware of what has been
happening. The episode that follows is also ironic: the shared
secret appears to work to the knight's advantage in that he is
able to ask the duke where the chastelaine is, and he finds
himself ushered into the chamber 'por leenz entr'eus solacier'
(l.859). The reality that confronts him is in grim opposition to
that envisaged by the duke.

The tragic dénouement moves swiftly since both the knight
and the duke realize instantly the consequences of their
respective betrayals of the secret, and only the witness of the
servant girl is needed before suicide and then murder are
committed. Before dying the knight finally emerges as a tragic
figure through a monologue, as did the chastelaine before her
death. The description of the deaths of the three characters is

sufficiently detailed to provide a gruesome and dramatic out-come which is perhaps more in keeping with a *roman d'aventures* than a *lai*. The earlier ironic contrast is echoed in line 924 where we are reminded of the continuing festivities. It is here that the lovers' secret is disclosed one more time, as events are explained to the assembled company. The placing of the lovers in a single coffin and the departure of the duke offer two further opportunities for the perpetuating of their story.

Thus we are brought to the epilogue and, as we have already seen, this is closely linked to the prologue, with its stress on the theme of secrecy and its opposite, *li descouvrirs*. While con-tinuing as a *leitmotif*, irony has given way to tragedy, and a general moral is drawn from particular circumstances. The story comes full circle in the reference to those 'qui enquierent autrui amors' (l.958), for, as we have seen, these may be people who share with *fin amant* the ability to love (as does the duke) and conceal feelings (as does the duchess), yet who cause the tragic end of lovers. The only answer is the seemingly impossible *amor celer* (l.952).

2. *La Chastelaine de Vergi:* Traditional Themes and Motifs

The author of *La Chastelaine de Vergi* uses traditional material at every stage in his story. There is, of course, nothing at all unusual in this, for in the Middle Ages a successful literary technique consisted, to a large extent, of the interweaving of familiar motifs. If this is clearly discernible in much twelfth-century writing, it has been suggested that such allusiveness is even more characteristic of the early thirteenth century. Lakits (*13*, p.30) refers to 'un penchant de plus en plus fort pour le *conventionnel*, tendance qui s'explique essentiellement par la sclérose de la civilisation courtoise, se retranchant dans sa singularité'. This is not to say that all medieval writing is wholly derivative, but rather that originality lay in the way in which recognized themes and motifs were combined and developed. In this chapter, then, we shall be concerned with isolating these themes and examining their treatment in important aspects of the text: characterization, the 'Potiphar's wife' episode, the lovers' secret meetings, the heroine's laments and the tragic ending.

(i) *Characterization*

The composition of *La Chastelaine de Vergi* has been described as the 'marriage between two ostensibly incompatible genres', the combination of narrative intrigue and a situation typical of lyric poetry (Shirt, *18*, p.81), and this duality is reflected to some extent in the characters of the poem. The lovers themselves obviously stand in the line of ideal courtly lovers — *fin amant* — and this is indicated both by the way in which they are described and by explicit comparison with the great lovers of legend (a device which is already a cliché of courtly poetry):

> 'Je cuidoie que plus loiaus
> me fussiez, se Dieus me conseut,
> que ne fust Tristans a Yseut'
>   (ll.758-60)

On the other hand, the duke and duchess do not conform to such stereotypes and belong rather to a narrative tradition; the temptress figure represented by the duchess is already to be found in twelfth-century *lais* of the *grand roman courtois* type, as we shall see later, which also combine narrative and lyric elements.

In introducing the two lovers to his audience, the author of *La Chastelaine de Vergi* draws extensively on the conventions of courtly love, but with his own particular purpose, that of presenting a well-established love affair. For although there are many courtly allusions in the poem, the essential feature of courtly tradition is missing: we do not see the characters fall in love with each other. There is no description of love coming into being (the *amour naissant* beloved of Marie de France and others), nor of the qualities demanded of the lovers: their respective merits, persistence in the face of adversity, and so on. This, then, already represents a deviation from courtly lyric poems, which are more usually concerned with the lover's attempts to woo his lady, and from those stories of chivalry where the lover dedicates himself to seeking adventure, to the same end. The omission is a telling one; had the author chosen to describe his characters falling in love he would have been constrained to reveal much more about them, and perhaps to explain that need for secrecy which is at the heart of his story. As it is, this results in a further omission, noted in the previous chapter, which breaks still further with strict courtly tradition: the figure of a jealous husband is absent, and his actual existence becomes questionable.

Therefore since we have no account of the beginning of the lovers' relationship, many details of characterization are overlooked, and the author relies on tradition to fill the gaps. The fact that the love affair conforms to the ideals of courtly love is established in the generalities of the prologue. The crucial con-

cept of loyalty is referred to in the second line, to be followed by
the convention of secrecy (1.3), a reference to *joie* (1.9) and to *li
fin amant* themselves (1.12). These courtly prerequisites are then
associated with one particular couple, and we are left in no
doubt as to the nature of their love.

There is no description at all of the chastelaine, either at the
beginning of the poem, or later when the duke observes her
meeting her lover, except for the minor physical detail of 'ses
biaus braz' in line 401. This is not particularly unusual, for the
troubadours who were preoccupied with the emotions of the
lover often took the lady's perfection for granted, not troubling
to describe it. But it does contrast with the fairly widespread use
of a formalized 'portrait' technique, perfected by Chrétien de
Troyes, where the lady's attributes were enumerated in a set
pattern. Indeed, it is only after the lady's death that the familiar
adjectives of courtly description are used at any length, in the
knight's lament:

> 'Ha! las! dist il, ma douce amor
> la plus cortoise et le meillor
> c'onques fust et la plus loial...'
> (ll.885-87)

Her lover does not fare much better; in line 19 he is said simply
to be 'preu et hardi' — adjectives typically applied to any courtly
lover. His courtliness is, however, indicated by the fact that the
duchess, a woman who is clearly his social superior, also falls in
love with him. That episode begins with a couple of lines
describing his comeliness and his valour:

> Li chevaliers fu biaus et cointes,
> et par sa valor fu acointes
> du duc qui Bourgoingne tenoit
> (ll.43-45)

Then the duchess begins her attempted seduction of him with the
words

> 'Sire, vous estes biaus et preus,
> ce dient tuit, la Dieu merci...'
>
> (ll.60-61)

thereby adding the detail of his renown. With only this negligible amount of personal detail, the lovers are evoked instead in terms of their great love for each other:

> que li chevaliers tant ama
> que la dame li otria...
>
> (ll.21-22)

and this, following the courtly allusions of the prologue, is sufficient to convey their suitability as a courtly couple.

Despite the absence of descriptive detail, the unmistakable characterization of the lovers as courtly, right from the outset of the poem, prepares us in part for the way in which they will behave as the action develops. As far as the other two characters of the duke and duchess are concerned, we have no such expectations. We are given no physical description or background details of them, and have to observe them entirely through their words and actions. It is a tribute to the skill of the author that these characters quickly emerge as credible and interesting. Admittedly he is helped by the existence of comparable characters in literary tradition, but such references are less obvious and less crucial than the courtly allusions in the case of the lovers.

In discussing the character of the duke, Lakits (*13*, pp.72-73) speaks of 'l'étonnante originalité de ce personnage', 'la richesse nuancée de son caractère', and even goes so far as to suggest that he is the true tragic hero of the story. Similarly, Zumthor, discussing the role of the duke as the surviving witness to events, suggests that 'peut-être, en ce sens, la figure du duc est-elle centrale dans l'œuvre' (*20*, p.253). Frappier (*11*, p.100) sees the duke as the only character who does not conform to a common type, and it is certainly true that there is no exact parallel to be found. Instead it is possible to discern several different character types which are welded together in an original whole.

The duke has a double function with respect to the knight. First and foremost he is his feudal overlord who not only commands the service and respect of his vassal but also honours the feudal obligation with deep affection. Thus when his wife slanders the knight the duke is distressed, not for his wife's sake, but because of the implications for his vassal:

> A malaise fu cele nuit
> li dus, n'onques dormir ne pot
> por le chevalier qu'il amot...
>
> (ll.144-46)

While there are examples in medieval literature of jealousy and hatred in the relationship between lord and vassal, the motif of a loving and sympathetic relationship is a commonplace from the *Chanson de Roland* onwards. Secondly, however, the relationship between duke and knight transcends the formal one and becomes one of pure friendship. Despite the onus that is on the knight to disprove the duchess's allegations, the duke never displays any hostility towards him. As the two set out together for the castle of Vergi the feudal relationship is easily forgotten.

This motif of the lover and his companion is again familiar, particularly from courtly romance where, often, the companion would be paired off with the lady's confidante. The example that springs most readily to mind is that of Tristan's friend Kaherdin who, in Thomas's *Roman de Tristan*, requires to see Tristan's mistress in order to be convinced that his sister (Tristan's wife in his unconsummated marriage) has not been slighted by her husband's neglect. There, as in *La Chastelaine de Vergi*, the friend has a vested interest in observing the lovers. More generally, in the episode where the lovers spend the night together while the duke remains outside, the duke is reminiscent of the lover's friend in the Provençal *alba*, whose function it was to guard the lovers and warn them when the night was over.

Then the duke, who is the knight's friend and overlord, has a third role to play, that of husband to a woman who is characterized by her wrongdoing. The very nature of the episode (see pp.32-35 below) creates its own parallel figures, but perhaps it is also legitimate to look beyond the 'Potiphar's wife' theme for character types. While the king in the same situation in *Lanval* is, according to Lakits, just 'an anonymous force' (*13*, p.72), King Arthur in *La Mort le Roi Artu* offers a closer likeness. Like the duke in *La Chastelaine de Vergi*, Arthur loves his wife, yet he is prepared to sacrifice her when the forces of law are joined against her. The idea that a husband shall carry out the demands of justice on his wife, overruling his previous love for her, is also to be found in Marie de France's poems *Equitan* and *Bisclavret*. Thus the three separate facets of the duke each have their precursors, while the full character of the man corresponds to none of them. Above all a man of great integrity, whose 'weakness' is in upholding his marriage vows rather than betraying his friend, he is indeed the most original and interesting of the four.

More than the other three, the character of the duchess emerges in the light of the literary counterparts to the main episode in which she figures — her attempt to seduce the knight and her slander of him. But, as with her husband, certain aspects of her character reflect a wider background, in particular that of the courtly lyric. Thus immediately she is presented the author takes care to stress, by unmistakable repetition of a key term, that through one failing in her love or desire (although not elsewhere in the poem), that is the inability to hide her feelings, she is behaving in an uncourtly fashion:

> ... la duchoise l'enama
> et li fist tel *samblant* d'amors
> que, s'il n'eüst le cuer aillors,
> bien se peüst apercevoir
> par *samblant* que l'amast por voir.
> Mes quel *samblant* qu'el en feïst
> li chevaliers *samblant* n'en fist
> que poi ne grant n'aperceüst
> qu'ele vers li amor eüst ....
> (ll.48-56, my italics)

This lack of discretion is reflected in her taking the initiative and

propositioning the knight. Although Lakits (*13*, p.74) maintains
that her approach is discreet and that she retains 'un vernis de
courtoisie' throughout the ensuing dialogue, I feel that it is the
impression of uncourtliness that predominates, as she rejects the
knight's courteous replies and becomes increasingly angry, and
in this she resembles the spurned queen in *Lanval* in a parallel
situation.

When the duke is persuaded to betray the lovers' secret, the
duchess in conversation with her husband is reminiscent of other
women in medieval literature who take advantage of their
husband's love to coax them into unintended revelations. The
duchess's speech and behaviour in lines 597ff. again recall the
lady in *Bisclavret*, and, despite the thematic differences between
the two poems, the duke and duchess in *La Chastelaine de Vergi*
do have a certain amount in common with the married couple in
Marie's *lai*.

Thus of the four characters in the story, two, the lovers, are
defined in terms of the courtly tradition of *fin amor*, while a
third, the duchess, falls within the same category through being
characterized by her opposition to the lovers. Frappier sees her
as representing the *losengiers* — 'une transposition féminine qui
n'est pas rare au XIIIe siècle' (*11*, p.100). The interest inherent
in the character of the duke, on the other hand, perhaps reflects
the wider range of traditions underlying this figure.

(ii) *The 'Potiphar's Wife' episode*

Apart from a brief reference to the way in which the lovers
meet (ll.29-39) the first important action in *La Chastelaine de
Vergi* is the so-called 'Potiphar's wife' episode. It is introduced
simply by the detail that the lovers had maintained secrecy for a
long time (ll.40-43), a further move away from the traditional
stress on courtship in courtly literature. The name commonly
given to this theme refers to the story recounted in Genesis 39:
6ff., where the wife of Joseph's master, having tried repeatedly
to seduce Joseph without success, accuses him of having
approached her instead, and Joseph is thrown into prison.
Critics have related the Genesis story both to *La Chastelaine de*

Vergi and to Marie de France's *lai* of *Lanval*, but it would be misguided to try to draw too close a parallel between the Biblical narrative and the medieval texts: when the details are considered there are inevitably important differences. For example the Old French stories have their heroes tempted on just a single occasion, whereas Joseph was pestered many times; in *Lanval* and *La Chastelaine de Vergi* the knight is given a chance to disprove the accusation, whereas Joseph is punished without a hearing. This second difference would no doubt be necessary to satisfy the desire for justice in a feudal society, and it is sufficient to see the general idea of 'the temptress rebuffed' as the traditional theme underlying this episode, with the details varying according to the purpose of the story.

In *La Chastelaine de Vergi* the 'temptress' is ultimately punished, although not directly, for the slander she inflicted. Instead she is killed for having betrayed the secret entrusted to her. In *Lanval*, on the other hand, there is no reference to the queen's fate once the hero has acquitted himself, for it is only incidental to the main thrust of the story. If we are to seek a precedent for the death of the duchess we could go back to the Ancient Egyptian 'Story of the two brothers', which is thought to have influenced the tale in Genesis. This is the story of a woman who falsely accuses her husband's younger brother; however, the man chooses to believe his brother's rather dramatic protestations of innocence and kills his wife. This is clearly one of the great themes of mythology and could be traced back still further. It is not therefore surprising to find it recurring, with inevitable modifications of detail, in Western medieval literature, although whether the author was aware of its sources is debatable.

If we leave aside the question of parallels between the episode in *La Chastelaine de Vergi* and other works such as *Lanval* (see further *10* and *14*), the scene between the duchess and the knight reflects various aspects of the twelfth-century courtly tradition. The duchess begins by suggesting that the knight is worthy

> '... d'avoir amie en si haut leu
> qu'en eüssiez honor et preu ...'
>
> (ll.63-64)

which echoes the courtly notion that a knight is ennobled by his love and may therefore aspire to love a lady who is his social superior. The knight's polite reply takes up the idea of class difference, suggesting that such a relationship is not practicable:

> '... ne je sui ne duc ne conte
> que si hautement amer doie...'
>
> (ll.76-77)

This aspect of the courtly code had already been criticized in Marie de France's *Equitan* which demonstrated the unfortunate consequences of an adulterous relationship where the partners were of unequal standing. This obsession with nuances of social class obviously contributes to the duchess's fury when she discovers that the knight has rejected her for someone of lower rank (ll.660ff.).

In the next stage of the story, when the knight rejects the duchess, on the pretext of loyalty to his overlord, we find, for the first time in *La Chastelaine de Vergi*, the language of courtly love used with its customary ambiguity. When the knight declines to

> '... fere desreson
> si vilaine et si desloial
> vers mon droit seignor natural.'
>
> (ll.96-98)

he is using adjectives — *vilaine*, *desloial* — which may refer both to feudal disloyalty and to uncourtly behaviour in love, and such ambiguity, widely exploited in courtly literature, obviously adds a further dimension to the text. It is echoed by the duchess when she promptly complains to the duke of those who are *trahitor* (l.118).

We have already seen how the duchess is able to manipulate her husband into doing what she wants, and I have already suggested a parallel with the *lai* of *Bisclavret*, where a man of integrity is married to a less scrupulous wife. There remain two further points that emerge from the final part of this 'Potiphar's wife' episode. When the knight has proved his innocence to the duke's satisfaction, the theme of discretion is resumed, and this time it is the duke who unwittingly begins the betrayal of the lovers' secret through his *samblant* — his facial expression:

> Et cel jor quant vint au mengier
> moustra li dus au chevalier
> plus biau samblant qu'ainz n'avoit fait...
> (ll.509-11)

Here we may be reminded of Marie de France's *Yonec*, where the lady is unable to control her features sufficiently to hide the change in her brought about by having a lover, and this subtle form of indiscretion finds expression in *La Chastelaine de Vergi* not in a lover but in a friend. Then, secondly, the duchess's reaction to the knight's reinstatement is like that of the queen in *Lanval* — she goes to bed with a headache. The difference is that in *Lanval* it is the queen's reaction to the earlier stage in events, her rejection by the hero.

Thus the author's portrayal of the first stage in the action uses the same technique as in his presentation of characters. There are recognizable general parallels with earlier literature — in the use of character 'types' and in a particular event — but there are also subsidiary details which derive instead from various aspects of courtly tradition.

(iii) *The secret rendez-vous*

In some respects the account of the lovers' meeting (ll.374-487) emphasizes the divergence from tradition, reminding us that the story begins with an established relationship. The meeting is simply one of many — not the first nor necessarily the last. It is significant solely because the duke is an unseen witness. The lovers' feelings and behaviour are no different from any other occasion. Thus the episode recounted in lines 400-18 bears some resemblance to Marie de France's *Chèvrefoil*, which describes a single meeting between the exiled Tristan and Queen Iseut, although in this case we have far more information available, the familiar details of the Tristan legend.

The importance of the way in which such a meeting is arranged is indicated by the fact that the details are given in advance in the introductory section:

> deviserent qu'en un vergier
> li chevaliers toz jors vendroit
> au terme que li meteroit,
> ne se mouveroit d'un anglet
> de si que un petit chienet
> verroit par le vergier aler.
>
> (ll.30-35)

When the duke questions the knight about this — 'comment savez lieu ne tens?' (l.351) — the knight mentions the dog in particular: '... du petit chien la maniere' (l.358). The dog in fact assumes a crucial role in the course of the poem, not just through its basic function of alerting the lover, but because later in the poem it has become symbolic of the fact that they meet. So when the duke has told his wife the details of the lovers' rendez-vous (ll.652-55), it takes no more than a reference to the dog for the chastelaine to realize that she has been betrayed. In just three lines of speech the duchess destroys the secret:

> 'mais vous estes bone mestresse,
> qui avez apris le mestier
> du petit chienet afetier'
>
> (ll.716-18)

Similarly when the lover and the duke are told the story of the chastelaine's death the betrayal hinges on the detail of the dog:

> '... ma dame l'ataïna
> et d'un chienet la ramposna ...'
>
> (ll.879-80)

and

si qu'ele n'i a riens teü,
comment l'afere ert commencié,
neïs du chienet afetié
dont la duchoise avoit parlé.

(ll.906-09)

In this account of the secret rendez-vous there are a number of traditional motifs. In particular the dog has literary parallels in the use of both animals and humans by lovers for communicating with each other. In Marie de France's *Milun* it is a swan who carries messages between the lovers and comes to symbolize their enduring relationship. In *Chèvrefoil* it is a stick of ash that reveals Tristan's presence to Iseut. The little dog is unmistakably reminiscent of the dog Husdent, in Béroul's *Tristran* and in the *Folie d'Oxford*, who was given by Tristan to Iseut and is able to recognize his master when his mistress is deceived by her lover's disguise. More commonly, though, the secret is shared with a maid or manservant acting as a go-between, and this is what the duke anticipates in line 346. At the end of *La Chastelaine de Vergi* the dog's function is indeed taken over by the more familiar figure of a maidservant. The *pucelete* who unintentionally witnesses the chastelaine's lament and death is a necessary adjunct for the truth of the story to be made known, although her presence is inevitably somewhat contrived. Maraud has suggested a close similarity between the girl and the dog. Like the animal she comprehends nothing and transmits a message she does not understand. Just as the dog is the 'stratagème des amants', so the maid is a 'stratagème du récit' (*14*, p.455).

The setting of the rendez-vous draws extensively on motifs from lyric poetry. Typically, the scene is set in a place apart, in this case an orchard (ll.30, 381, 652), which is reminiscent of the first fragment of Thomas's *Roman de Tristan*. (It has, incidentally, been suggested that this motif of the orchard was responsible for the title of *La Châtelaine du verger* given to some later versions of the story, once the castle of Vergi had been ruined and forgotten.) The orchard is said to be in a garden (l.378) and this recalls the theme of an enclosed garden, which formerly could have magical connotations, although this is neither the case here nor, for instance, in Marie de France's *Guigemar*. Similar overtones are associated with its alternative designation as a meadow (l.395), which was, for example, the setting for Lanval's first meeting with his fairy mistress (*Lanval*, l.44). Finally, the lovers' ultimate place of secrecy is the lady's bedroom where she awaits his arrival in the garden. The watching duke can only hear what is being said before they go inside, and the fact that they cannot be observed is conveyed by the author's use of a digression to cover their absence.

Apart from these easily recognizable motifs of the *verger*, *prael* and *chambre*, the lovers' greetings reflect the language of lyric poetry. A long-established relationship is reflected in the order of events:

> ... et plus de cent fois le besa
> ainz que feïst longue parole
> (ll.403-04)

whereas in a poem concerned with *amour naissant* the reverse is to be expected. The opening words of knight and lady convey the lovers' equality through a somewhat contrived parallelism, using the forms of address of the courtly lyric. '"Ma dame, m'amie / m'amor, mon cuer, ma druerie..."' begins the knight (ll.405-06) and his mistress replies: '"Mon douz seignor, / mes druz amis, ma douce amor..."' (ll.411-12). The whole episode of the secret rendez-vous is one which perhaps owes most to courtly lyric tradition, as the use of such language suggests, but it should be borne in mind that the dog at least is not a gratuitous motif, but an important element in the structure of the story.

(iv) *The heroine's lament and the tragic ending*

The picture of a lady lamenting her dead or dying lover is a familiar one in medieval literature. At the end of the *Roman de Tristan*, for example, the ideal courtly lover dies because of the apparent absence of his beloved, and, after lamenting him, Iseut soon joins him in death. A similar situation, although expressed in less courtly terms, provides the tragic end to *Pyrame et Thisbé*. In *La Chastelaine de Vergi*, while the mode of expression is courtly, the situation is slightly different: the heroine in lines 733-831 laments the presumed death not of her lover but of his love.

The main theme of the lament, once the chastelaine has expressed her mistaken assumption that the knight loves the duchess (ll.733-44) is the strength of her own love. It draws on courtly vocabulary and rhetorical devices, but without being unduly elevated in tone. Linguistically, therefore, there is little that is unexpected in this passage, although, predictably, the author does vary the context of some traditional features. For instance, in lines 750-52 the chastelaine enumerates six abstract nouns which are key terms in courtly vocabulary and uses them metonymically of her lover:

> 'Quar c'ert ma joie et mon deduit,
> c'ert mes delis, c'ert mes depors,
> c'ert mes solaz, c'ert mes confors.'[1]

Although such usage is not in any way deviant these forms in the lyric are more likely to be used by the lover of his lady, rather than the other way about. The same procedure is followed a little later:

> 'quar vous estiiez ma richece
> et ma santez et ma leece'
> (ll.779-80)

A rhetorical device used throughout the poem is particularly noticeable in this passage, that is the use of pairs of near synonyms. A good example of this is in the picture of the ideal lover that the knight has been (ll.791-98), and the traditional device is varied by the ironic associations provided by the context. Thus in the general lament

---

[1] Rhetorical figures occur throughout the text, for example the *accumulatio* used here, and the *annominatio* quoted on p.31 above.

> '... je ne penssaisse a nul fuer
> qu'il peüst trover en son cuer
> envers moi corouz ne haïne
> por duchoise ne por roïne
>
> (ll.793-96)

the virtual synonyms of line 796 assume a poignant significance. A little later she says:

> 'De lui me penssoie autressi
> qu'il se tenoit a mon ami
> toute sa vie et son eage'
>
> (ll.799-801)

and here the last synonyms emphasizing the idea of a lifelong love are ironic in view of the impending death of both lovers.

The heroine's death following this lament, while clearly reminiscent of that of other tragic lovers, is a shock. The indiscretion which is its root cause was such that our expectations remain geared to some kind of final intervention and explanation, following, perhaps, the example of *Lanval*. Yet the description of her death is couched in highly conventional terms and provokes the comment by Lakits: 'ce qui prouve... à quel point les auteurs courtois les plus originaux se conforment au canon dès qu'il s'agit de thèmes consacrés par la tradition' (*13*, p.93). This is, however, only true of a few lines (ll.835-39) of the final episode, and even here the author shows his originality by setting stereotyped description alongside a different context to produce an ironic contrast. Thus a description which is typical of the expression of suffering of various kinds in courtly writing,

> angoisseusement s'est pasmee,
> et gist pale et descoloree
>
> (ll.837-38)

is followed by a reference to the festivities in the hall and the lover's ignorance of her death. The lines are also ambiguous, as is shown by the lover's pathetic assumption that the chastelaine is alive, in spite of being 'descolorée et perse' (l.864). Conventional language contributes again to irony as the lover embraces the lady we know to be dead:

> Cil maintenant l'acole et baise
> qui bien en ot et lieu et aise
>
> (ll.865-66)

The suicide of the knight recalls the double suicide at the end of *Pyrame et Thisbé*, in particular the death of Thisbé, who falls across the body of her dying lover. Although the language of *La Chastelaine de Vergi* is richer in courtly allusion at this point (cf. ll.885-89), there are both narrative and linguistic parallels with the twelfth-century poem here. Then after the duke has avenged his friend's betrayal by killing his wife the two lovers are buried in a single coffin, a detail which is found in other tragic love stories, including *Pyrame et Thisbé* (following Ovid) and Marie de France's *Les Deus Amanz*. *La Chastelaine de Vergi* does, however, offer a slight variation on all these death scenes. In *Les Deus Amanz*, as in the *Roman de Tristan*, the lady apparently dies of a broken heart, while Thisbé kills herself at the sight of her dead lover. In *La Chastelaine de Vergi* these events are reversed: the lady dies of a broken heart at the idea of her lover's treachery, and he then kills himself with a convenient sword.

It may seem then that at virtually every stage in the story there is a parallel to be drawn with an episode from literary tradition, or that the language evokes the established conventions of courtly love. It this is so, why are we not faced with a text which is monotonously derivative, if not unreadable? I shall attempt to answer this in the next chapter by assessing the author's originality in blending together these diverse themes and motifs.

3. *La Chastelaine de Vergi:* Originality

(i) *Genre*

One thing a number of critics seem to agree upon is that *La Chastelaine de Vergi* displays a certain originality first of all with respect to genre. As we have already seen in Chapter One, despite a number of similarities with the twelfth-century *lai*, this text does not wholly conform to the established pattern. Thus Dubuis concludes that it is an 'œuvre mêlée' (*2*, p.525) — a work which is neither *lai* nor poem, neither *nouvelle* nor *roman*, but in some respects suggesting a transition from the *lai* to the *nouvelle*, while retaining many characteristics of the former. Zumthor equally seems to see this text as symptomatic of a development which leads up to the fifteenth-century *nouvelle*, and which also involves the related genres of *lais*, *fabliaux*, *contes* and so on. It is transitional in that 'l'auteur [de *La Chastelaine de Vergi*] entend à la fois faire œuvre narrative et se plier au goût courtois, mais néanmoins échapper à l'esthétique impliquée par le "roman"' (*20*, p.251). Several critics who have elaborated the parallels between *La Chastelaine de Vergi* and *Lanval* have been at pains to point out that this is not to deny originality to our text. In the words of Maraud: 'Si deux textes semblent apparentés, l'originalité de l'un n'est certes pas réductible à la somme de ses différences avec l'autre' (*14*, p.433). Although the structural differences between *La Chastelaine de Vergi* and the twelfth-century *lais* and *romans courtois* are not sufficiently clear-cut to talk of innovation, it is worth considering the stylistic effect of the formal characteristics of *La Chastelaine de Vergi* in the context of the work's originality.

There are three important formal differences between *La Chastelaine de Vergi* and, say, the *lai*: the lack of any clear structural division within the text corresponding to changes in scene, the absence of even the brief descriptive detail found elsewhere, and a near total indifference to passing time. It is not enough simply to attribute the lack of description, for example, to a corresponding lack of interest in character analysis in the thirteenth century, as does Zumthor (*20*, p.252). Instead we need to examine the stylistic effect of these omissions and this can be done very quickly.

As one might expect, the result of the story being unhindered by structural and temporal breaks and by descriptions is the impression of an extremely fast-moving narrative. I have already drawn attention to the difficulty of pinpointing the transitions from one section to another, and the same problem occurs if we try to demarcate specific episodes. This is due in part to the author's tendency, mentioned in Chapter One above, to include in one rhyming couplet the end of one episode and the beginning of the next. This is seen especially in small units, for example in the conversation between the duchess and the knight, where she is telling him that he should take a noble mistress:

> 'que bien vous serroit tele *amie*.
> — Ma dame, fet il, je n'ai *mie*
> encore a ce mise m'*entente*.
> — Par foi, dist ele, longue *atente*
> vous porroit nuire, ce m'est vis...'
> (ll.65-69; my italics)

Similarly the end of the knight's confession to the duke is linked to the latter's questions about the details of the lovers' meetings:

> '... j'aim vostre niece de Vergi,
> et ele moi, tant c'on puet plus.
> — Or me dites donc, fet li dus...
> (ll.342-44)

In this way the narrative is unfragmented and conversation flows freely, although the rhyme does not usually link more disparate elements (as it does, for instance, in *Le Lai de l'ombre*).

The lack of descriptive detail, either with regard to the characters or their setting also allows the author to concentrate

on the action itself. More significantly, it enables the characters
to emerge through their own words and actions, the result of
which is a very selective psychological picture. Dubuis's
comment, that 'La psychologie des personnages principaux est
très justement observée ... mais elle se limite aux seuls traits de
caractère qui commandent le déroulement de l'intrigue ou le
justifient' (2, pp.521-22) reflects this selectivity, without
attributing it exactly to the causes I have specified. In place of
descriptive passages we find dialogue and monologue used more
extensively, in proportion to the length of the text, than in
earlier short verse romances.

Finally the absence of virtually any expression of length of
time (*durée*) is interesting. There is just one occasion where we
have a traditional reference to passing time, but not at a place
where it can create a structural break. It occurs at line 682 where
we are told of the duchess's impatience to avenge herself on the
chastelaine:

> Mes ainc en point n'en lieu n'en vint
> tant que la Pentecouste vint
> qui aprés fu, a la premiere
> que li dus tint cort mout pleniere
>   (ll.681-84)

The time reference is almost incidental and does nothing to
disturb the flow of the narrative. Instead it adds to our knowledge of the character of the duchess who has harboured her
grudge and concealed her secret for, one supposes, quite a length
of time. Because time thus has no structural function in the
narrative, its use in relation to the emotions of the lovers is all
the more marked and effective. The most obvious example of
this is the author's digression to avoid describing the lovers'
night together. In this context periods of time are accumulated
to express the desire of a lover for time to be extended
indefinitely while he is with his beloved (ll.450-60). This
theoretical aside is, however, echoed in the thoughts and speech
of the lovers afterwards. Thus the knight remarks to the duke:
'trop li avoit duré petit' (l.482), while the chastelaine's lament

has the lines

> '... et je l'amoie tant
> comme riens peüst autre amer,
> qu'aillors ne pooie pensser
> nis une eure ne jor ne nuit!'
>
> (ll.746-49)

In this way the author succeeds in creating a narrative which is temporally self-contained, by eliminating references to time passing outside his story, and appropriates details of passing time to emphasize instead the emotions of his characters.

If, therefore, we can see in *La Chastelaine de Vergi* an original structure — an *œuvre mêlée* — with its own unity based on a continuous, circular structure, which lacks description and *durée*, we must next ask how the characters and events are presented and try to guage the extent of the author's originality in this respect.

(ii) *Content*

We have already hinted at a degree of originality in the details of events and characters in *La Chastelaine de Vergi* in the previous chapter, in a somewhat negative way, in considering the extent to which the narrative does not conform to traditional types and patterns. If we now look at certain aspects of the poem more positively — without reference to preceding works — further indications of the author's originality as regards content, technique and style come to light.

The author treats the events in his narrative as exemplary; he includes the term *example* (l.951) in his epilogue, which evokes the genre of didactic poetry common at the time. If his purpose is indeed primarily didactic it does not matter that some critics have found a certain irrationality in the events described. Dubuis even goes so far as to condemn the actual moral of the story as '[une leçon] bien plate et insipide' (*2*, p.521). Yet, as Whitehead puts it, 'few works with so artificial a plot as the *Chastelaine* leave a stronger impression of verisimilitude on the reader'

(Introduction, p.xlii), and this alone seems to constitute a facet of the author's originality. How is this impression of verisimilitude created?

First of all, we are clearly presented from the outset with a thoroughly realistic, full-blooded, happy love affair. It is important to note that although the outcome is a tragic one, there is, as Lakits points out (*13*, p.67), no overwhelming sense of fatality in the events preceding the heroine's suicide. Tragedy is introduced in the course of the story without any false air of either fateful inevitability or redemptive morality, in much the same way as the abbé Prévost was to bring tragedy into the novel in his *Manon Lescaut* five centuries later. Similarly, although the condition laid down by the chastelaine appears improbably stringent, this does not entail any unrealistic behaviour on the part of either of the lovers in the ways in which they attempt to safeguard their secret.

Two further points with respect to the basic situation of the lovers. First, it has been suggested that thirteenth-century realism is responsible for replacing the 'fairy mistress' of, for example, the *lai* of *Lanval*, by a thoroughly human lady, whose title is taken from real life. If this is so, I find it highly improbable (*pace* Reed, *16*, p.202, and others) that traditional details such as that of the private meeting in a garden and the oath of secrecy betray a fairy ancestry for the lady. She is human with respect to her sexuality, her perplexity in the face of the duchess's onslaught, and her impulsive (and irrational) emotional reaction to the disclosure of her secret. Secondly, as I have already commented, the lady's marital status is unclear. It is perhaps significant that some authors of later adaptations of *La Chastelaine de Vergi* have felt it necessary to be more explicit. In Marguerite de Navarre's *Heptaméron*, for example, the lady is said to be a widow, and elsewhere she is clearly stated to be unmarried (see further *16*, p.201). The important point to be borne in mind when reading the original is that the author assumes the logicality of the need for secrecy. Thus he achieves a realistic treatment of events, by not questioning his frame of reference and by not introducing any extraneous characters.

If we accept that in taking as a starting point an established love affair the author of *La Chastelaine de Vergi* is writing objectively and realistically, we must then ask where the true emphasis of the story is to be found. The actual process of falling in love is not in question, for, realistically enough, this does not entail any great 'adventure'. Arrathoon suggests (*10*, p.154) that it is the knight's dilemma which is 'the true core of the work', while Lakits denies the entire story any 'adventure': instead he argues that it centres on *mésaventure* — the loss of what a knight ought normally to gain by adventure (*13*, p.55). This latter view seems mistaken if we remember that Marie de France's *lais* had already established that any love-centred event, whether in the creation or destruction of a relationship, whether big or small, could justly be termed *aventure*. And if we need to seek a central event of this nature for *La Chastelaine de Vergi*, I suggest that it may be found in the climax of the three revelations, that is in the brief but crucial encounter between the two women, the chastelaine and the duchess, and its presentation may be regarded as a further instance of the author's original approach. The scene described in lines 698-722 is the inevitable result of the duchess's unsuccessful attempt to seduce the knight, and the direct cause of the double death that follows.

I have already discussed the characters of *La Chastelaine de Vergi* in some depth in the previous chapter, where we saw that it is the duke and duchess who are the more original creations, while the lovers are conditioned to some extent by the traditional courtly stereotypes. The originality of this author lies instead in the presentation of the lovers' speech and thoughts. Stuip comments: 'On pourrait presque parler d'une petite pièce de théâtre où les répliques et les monologues sont extrêmement importants' (*19*, p.67). We have already noted the rapid conversational exchanges and it is worth considering now the two monologues which precipitate firstly the knight's confession to the duke and secondly the heroine's suicide.

The two monologues are quite different in form. That of the knight is shorter (lines 268-311) and is presented in a mixture of indirect and free indirect speech which causes it to blend easily into the narrative. The chastelaine's lament, on the other hand, is 100 lines long (ll.733-834) and in being spoken aloud represents a clear break from the surrounding narrative. The knight's soliloquy arises directly out of the previous speech by the duke offering him a choice between revealing his secret or exile, as he realizes that either option entails the loss of his mistress. The use of the present tense links this section with the preceding conversation and constitutes a variation of standard indirect speech which characteristically uses imperfects. It also allows the reader more immediate access to the lover's thoughts. At line 291 the subordinate clauses of reported speech cease and it is unclear whether the comparison here with the chastelain de Couci is made by the knight or the narrator, but it is possible to see this as a move to free indirect speech (which dispenses with a verb of 'saying that' and subordination) to introduce the extraneous feature of a verse of a song. After this the narrative voice returns to present a summary of the dilemma and its effect of visible anguish. This in turn relates it to the next section as the duke comes back on the scene, a link which is made by the use of a rhyming couplet, the device already mentioned:

> ... si qu'il en a le vis moillié.
> Li dus n'en ot pas le cuer lié,
> qui pensse qu'il i a tel chose
> que reconnoistre ne li ose.
>
> (ll.311-14)

The use of a verse from a song of the Chastelain de Couci has been the subject of some critical comment. It is also quoted in the *Roman de la Violete* and has been cited in attempts to date the *Chastelaine de Vergi* (see Whitehead's Introduction, pp.ix-xii). But however fashionable it may have been to imitate the *Guillaume de Dôle* in this procedure of including lyrics from elsewhere, I agree with Zumthor (*20*, p.230ff.) that this verse is not merely ornamental but appears to have been chosen to fit the situation: 'La strophe citée est destinée à expliciter et... à justifier les sentiments ressentis par le chevalier' (p.231). The verse itself is a typical example of the courtly lyric and its vocabulary, which is completely standard, offers an interesting contrast with the language of *La Chastelaine de Vergi*. There are, nonetheless, several linguistic links with the context in which it now occurs (*solaz* in the second line echoes line 285 and *cuers* in the penultimate line looks forward to line 308), as well as the obvious thematic link of sorrow at separation. On a more practical level, it also serves to fill out a monologue which is based only on two easily stated possibilities. Frappier, however, sees this use of the verse as a sign of the author's originality, suggesting that it contributes towards the creation of a psychological perspective within the work (*11*, p.104).

The second monologue is linked to its context at the beginning and end, but, as I have already suggested, its tone forms a marked contrast with what has gone before. The chastelaine begins by echoing the words of the duchess and we are shown how she immediately draws the wrong conclusion from them:

> 'Ce ne set ele par nului,
> ce sai je bien, fors par celui
> qui j'amoie et trahie m'a...'
> (ll.737-39)

This notion of betrayal is emphasized by repetition (l.743, and cf. l.826) and leads into the lament proper at line 746. Such an insight into the passionate emotions of the lady which this section offers would have been unusual in the courtly lyric (where the man's feelings were all-important), at least before Marie de France, and might be seen as part of the later move towards greater realism. Most striking is the change in tense which conveys the irreversibility of the lady's hastily passed judgement. The tragedy of the situation is made apparent by a sudden use of appeals or references to God (ll.746, 762, 773, 777, 820, 834) and to death (*paradis*, l.776; *mort*, ll.820, 825 etc.). In line 826 the theme of betrayal is set alongside that of death, and the speech ends with the quasi-liturgical 'Douz amis, a Dieu vous commant!' (l.834). Thus the chastelaine's lament has a double function. It serves firstly as a comment on the nature of the lady, showing her to be highly emotional and blinded by her love. Secondly it has the very precise structural function of explicitly introducing tragedy into the story, as the vocabulary reveals, since hitherto we have had little more than hints of a tragic undertone to the poem.

Although the characters appear to speak for themselves in these monologues and conversations, the narrator's presence is also to be felt. As Rychner has pointed out (*17*), this has the main function of explaining the reason for the feelings demonstrated (cf. lines 147, 180, 276 and 427). His conclusion is that 'un narrateur omniscient, implicitement mais constamment présent, analyse les réactions psychologiques qu'il prête à ses personnages. Nous ne voyons ceux-ci qu'à travers l'écran de sa présence: entre eux et nous, pas de contact direct' (*17*, p.93). The narrative voice can also be used for dramatic effect. Thus the last line of the chastelaine's lament is separated from the rest and strongly emphasized by the two interposed lines:

> Atant se tut la chastelaine,
> fors qu'ele dist en souspirant,
> 'Douz amis, a Dieu vous commant!'
> (ll.832-34)

Before leaving this section of the story, there is a further aspect of the author's originality to be observed in the heroine's suicide. The literary motif of a *suicide amoureux* has been examined by Lefay-Toury (*4*) and it is interesting that in most works where this occurs the themes of love and death tend to be closely associated. In *La Chastelaine de Vergi*, however, as we have seen, this is not really the case. The same author also notes that before the thirteenth century at least there is no such suicide presented 'sans qu'il en ressorte, au moins implicitement... une morale ou une philosophie' (*4*, pp.206-07). Again this is debatable in *La Chastelaine de Vergi*, for while there is a moral to be drawn, it has little to do with the fact of suicide, and its religious or philosophical implications. The author is not so much claiming that life is impossible without love, as proclaiming the danger inherent in revealing that love. It is a social moral that we are being invited to draw, not an ethical one (cf. *13*, p.67).

(iii) *Style*

The language and style of *La Chastelaine de Vergi* have attracted relatively little attention. Both Stuip (*19*, p.67) and Frappier (*11*, p.105) use the word *sobre* of the author's language, while Zumthor (*20*, p.237) comments on the 'extrême simplicité' of his vocabulary, but without examining the linguistic bases for these judgements. The linguistic *sobriété* of *La Chastelaine de Vergi* seems to me to lie in its sparing use of courtly vocabulary and its freedom from the stylistic complexities of courtly composition that were emerging by the end of the twelfth century. This is no doubt due in part to the high proportion of dialogue in the text, to which the mannerisms and clichés of courtly writing are inappropriate. In the narrative sections, courtly vocabulary is used initially to establish the overall style of the work. Thus in the prologue and introduction we find the concepts of the *fin amant* (l.12) and the *joie* (l.9) of courtly love; then the descriptive terms applied to the knight are highly traditional — *preu, hardi* (l.19), *biaus, cointes* (l.43), as are those applied to love — *douce, celee* (l.41). From then on, however, these conventions are rarely used. Instead individual concepts are singled out at specific points in the story, with the basic terms relating to concealment and revelation occurring intermittently throughout. When the knight is propositioned by the duchess he attempts to discourage her by using the conventional vocabulary for opposition either to feudal duty (as here) or to love — *vilain, desloial, desreson* (ll.96-97). Gradually the concept of loyalty, first alluded to in line 2, comes to the fore, and this aspect of courtly vocabulary predominates in lines 159-200 and 577-86. The author's technique seems to lie in a highly selective use of courtly conventions, drawing on them individually where it is appropriate, but never allowing the fundamentally unreal world of courtliness to take precedence over the realistic movement of the action. A similar conclusion is implied by Shirt's study (*18*) which notes clusters of key words (all of them basic terms in the courtly vocabulary) at certain points in the text. This is seen as creating harmony and balance within the poem, an effect which is held to be reinforced by the repetition or similarity of lines in different episodes (although what is repeated seems not to be very significant).

Against this general linguistic background the author of *La Chastelaine de Vergi* introduces, equally sparingly, occasional rhetorical devices, and in much the same way. As Lakits notes: 'Il le fait d'une manière tellement discrète qu'ils [les procédés] conservent toute leur valeur expressive' (*13*, p.91). The effect of this, according to Lakits, is important: it allows scenes to be differentiated because of a change in register, and adds a solemn character to apparently lyrical episodes. He does not cite passages to illustrate this, but my own interpretation of the language of *La Chastelaine de Vergi* outlined below tends to support his view, and indicates a further dimension to the author's originality.

The device which occurs most often is the use of pairs of synonyms for emphatic effect, and again they tend to be grouped in particular parts of the text. The first instance of this is in the duke's first speech to the knight threatening him with exile. The traditional form of a synonymic pair linked by a coordinator is to be found in line 172:

'... et la vous *vé et desfent* toute'

However, such is the emotion of the speaker and the gravity of the injunction that further synonyms have already occurred in the two preceding lines:

'*Issiez* errant hors de ma terre!
quar je vous en *congié* sans doute ...'
(ll.170-71)

In the ensuing conversation this device occurs again in the speech of the duke, in reporting his wife's accusations against the knight:

'cele meïsme conté m'a
en quel maniere et *en quel guise*
vous l'avez *proïe* et *requise*'
(ll.198-200)

This is not so much to characterize the duke as being particularly elegant in his speech as to depict the moments of tension, and synonymy is used again almost immediately in the narrative comment on the knight as

> Cil qui tout *covoite et desire*
> a geter son seignor de l'ire
> (ll.225-26)

and in seeking to exonerate himself:

> qu'il *ne pensse* ne *ne regarde*
> de ce dont li dus se prent garde
> (ll.233-34)

The same technique is used later on to present the duchess wheedling the secret out of her husband. Synonyms occur both in the narrative and in speech:

> — De ce que cil vous a conté,
> fet ele, *mençonge et arvoire*,
> qu'il vous a fet *pensser et croire*.
> (ll.594-96)

The greatest concentration of synonyms, however, is in the narrative following the heroine's suicide, while her lament is marked by the accumulation of related ideas (e.g. ll.750-52 and 779-80) rather than by the less spontaneous device of synonymy. The irony already noted in this episode is thus increased by the use of an emotive stylistic device, when the characters are as yet unaware of the emotional potential of the scene, e.g.

> au chevalier *commande et rueve*
> qu'en la garderobe la quiere
> (ll.856-57)

and

> Cil maintenant l'acole et baise,
> qui bien en ot et et *lieu et aise*
>
> (ll.865-66)

It is nonetheless important to bear in mind that at no time does the author of *La Chastelaine de Vergi* use synonymy to the extent that Chrétien de Troyes does, for example. Like the courtly vocabulary it occurs intermittently to emphasize a dominant emotion or tense situation and its context needs to be considered carefully. Nor is its use really sufficient to justify the assumption that different registers of the language are being exploited. There is little more than a hint of rhetorical style, which is limited almost entirely to synonymy, and this is not confined to any one character or episode. Even so, the regular association of synonymy with tension and its non-occurrence elsewhere constitute a further suggestion of originality.

Finally, the use of irony in *La Chastelaine de Vergi* needs to be borne in mind in assessing any claim of originality for the author. We have already seen how irony should be regarded as an integral part of the poem's structure, and this depends on what Rossman defines as 'the incongruous use of certain themes appreciated by the medieval reader' (*6*, p.95). In the case of *La Chastelaine de Vergi* it is the theme of ideal secrecy which is incongruous in the real world, in a way that discretion in *Lanval* is not. In addition we find examples of what Rossman terms 'episodic irony' (e.g. in the knight embracing his dead mistress), as well as verbal irony. Yet again *La Chastelaine de Vergi* seems to constitute a deviation from the norm of courtly romance.

It is obviously impossible to be dogmatic about what is or is not 'original' in any given literary text. In this chapter I have attempted to bring together a number of distinctive features in *La Chastelaine de Vergi* which in combination go to make up a work which is clearly not a routine re-telling of a story in accordance with predetermined literary conventions. Inevitably it is only the more distinctive works that have in any case survived the passage of time, and most have some claim to originality. Thus in moving on to *Le Lai de l'ombre* in the next chapter we shall be considering a wholly different arrangement of some of the features of technique and style which we have seen in *La Chastelaine de Vergi*, along with some others, and which in turn may justly be termed original.

4. Le Lai de l'ombre: Narrative and Ambiguity

Until quite recently critical comment on *Le Lai de l'ombre* had been mainly devoted to textual and editorial questions. As for the composition of the *lai* itself, this has been most commonly dismissed, albeit with some admiration, as a cameo or miniature, 'une historiette tendre et spirituelle' (Bédier, quoted by Lejeune-Dehousse, *27*, p.239). Nothing much happens, there is no *aventure* (Levy and Hindley, Introduction, p.viii). This, I believe, seriously undervalues the narrative, for if we view *Le Lai de l'ombre* in terms of the genre established by Marie de France, with its definition of love-related adventure, we find that there is indeed an event of some significance: love is pledged by the giving and receiving of a ring. Renart himself appears to see his work in these terms, stating that his intention is 'une aventure metre en rime' (l.45). The manner in which this is achieved seems to be unique, there being no known literary parallel, and the story is presented through narrative and dialogue which are rich in psychological interest.

There have been several attempts to portray *Le Lai de l'ombre* as being something other than a simple romance. Stevens argues that 'it serves the same general ends ... as Andreas Capellanus's *De Amore*' (*7*, p.192) and may have been formulated in reply to a question such as 'what should a knight do if his lady requires him to take back a ring which he has given her' (*loc.cit.*). Similarly Sargent (*28*) has seen a resemblance to the dialogues of the *De Amore* and labels the *Lai* a *contrasto* — an amorous dialogue. Both critics, however, go on to suggest that the *Lai* transcends the narrow limits they have set for it, and we are brought back to the idea of a peculiarly distinctive *lai*. This seems to be the conclusion reached too by Payen who says:

> *Le Lai de l'ombre* est autre chose qu'un art d'aimer; il apparaît d'abord comme la version courtoise d'un thème

de fabliau: celle du trompeur trompé, ou plutôt du
séducteur séduit. Il démontre ... les limites du discours
courtois et dénonce le rêve impossible des troubadours.

(*5*, p.185)

In this chapter I should like first to examine the narrative shape
of the *Lai*, and then to concentrate particularly on its inherent
ambiguity. It is this — the double meanings that arise out of the
characters, their speech and their behaviour — which seems to
me to mislead commentators into searching for remote sources
and literary influences.

Like the author of *La Chastelaine de Vergi*, Jean Renart
obscures structural divisions within the text by the use of
rhyming couplets which bridge divisions (see the examples on
p.43 above). This is a regular feature of *Le Lai de l'ombre*, as
opposed to its intermittent occurrence in the former work, and
the result is a flowing, seemingly unbroken, narrative. There is,
however, a carefully balanced structure discernible beneath this
surface regularity. Following the convention of the *lai*, the work
begins with a prologue setting out the author's intentions
(ll.1-52) and ends with a short epilogue (ll.952-62). The limits of
each are very clearly marked. The prologue, which is more the
length of a prologue to a long *roman*, or to a collection of
poems, than of one to a single poem, ends with three lines introducing the story and including its title: '... et dirai ci, du Lay de
l'ombre' (l.52). The epilogue is set apart from the preceding
narrative by a reference to the author himself in its second line:
'Jehan Renart a lor afere!' (l.953), and it also ends by including
the title again in its final couplet (ll.961-62). Despite this
precision Renart tells us nothing about the origin of his story
(although there is a passing reference to his informant in lines
390-91) and he himself has been described as 'a ghost who leaves
no tangible evidence of his presence where he has passed' (*22*,
p.17).

If we set aside these two sections we find that the main
narrative may be divided into two, with each part having its own
internal balance. The first part, from line 53 to 579 comprises
one narrative section (ll.53-324), in which the characters are

presented and the knight meets the lady face to face, and one
dialogue between them (ll.325-579). These subsections are of
almost equal length and, thematically, there appears to be a
complete break after part one, as the knight takes leave of the
lady:

> 'Dame', fet il, 'a vo congié!
> Sachiez que mon pooir et gié
> est toz en vo conmandement.'
>   (ll.577-79)

This air of finality is, of course, an illusion, but it is only in the
next section that it is revealed to the lady that the knight has left
his ring on her finger. The formal units are thus closely linked,
for the dialogue must inevitably be resumed quickly. In the
shorter part two there is a ternary pattern of episodes. In the
first section (ll.580-705) the characters are again apart, and the
most important feature is the lady's monologue as she considers
the ring on her finger and decides to call the knight back. Next,
in lines 706-827, we have the second dialogue, and finally, in
lines 828-51, there is the knight's monologue leading up to the
pledge of his love (in throwing the ring into the well) and its
acceptance by the lady. Part two, then, is more varied than part
one in that a third form of discourse — monologue — is added
to, and combined with, dialogue and narrative; action, hitherto
limited to coming and going, becomes crucial as the monologues
and dialogues give way to the final decisive gesture.

It is against this background of a formal structure which is to
some extent disguised by the rhyme scheme that I should like to
consider the components of the *Lai* and their ambiguity. This
will mean examining especially the characters and their
behaviour, but it is also worth bearing in mind that the literary
convention of courtliness on which the composition depends
may itself be regarded as having several layers of meaning. As
John Fox says of this work:

> The situation has all the ambiguity of courtly love, for it
> carries a hint of adultery; but over the whole relationship is

cast a cloak of good manners and *savoir-vivre*, for both knight and lady follow the recognized and accepted code of behaviour. (*3*, p.213)

Furthermore we shall see that, like the author of *La Chastelaine de Vergi*, Renart applies his own variations to the courtly tradition, and this creates further emotional and linguistic ambiguity.

It is an obvious fact of language that abstract terms are more ambiguous than words with just a few precise connotations, and we shall see in due course that a striking characteristic of Renart's style is his use of abstract nouns. Conversely, the least ambiguous nouns in any language are proper names. It is thus significant that there are no proper names in *Le Lai de l'ombre* and the two protagonists are not even given a rank or title, an anonymity which Adler (*21*, p.2) calls 'la direction vers l'immatériel'. Not only is the first character presented merely as 'uns chevaliers' (l.53), with the author facetiously disclaiming any knowledge of his name (ll.62-63), but the setting of the story is not much more precise:

> ... uns chevaliers iere
> en cele marche de l'Empiere
> de Loheraingne et d'Alemaingne
> (ll.53-55)

The period too is unspecified; whereas Marie de France's *lais* are all set in the distant past, the time here might be the present or any stage in the past. A vague allusion to the time of Arthurian romance may be seen in the comparisons made between the hero and Gauvain (ll.60-61) and with Tristan (ll.105, 124), but these references relate primarily to the presentation of the hero and only incidentally to time. With such abstractions made of the main elements of plot it is not hard to see how a variety of interpretations may emerge.

This shadowy background, against which the conversations between hero and heroine stand out in sharp relief, also absorbs the minor characters. Thus the heroine's husband is the subject of a polite allusion:

> '...j'ai mon seignor molt preudome
> qui molt me sert bien et enneure'
>   (ll.494-95)

The standard form of this description provokes the knight's sardonic reply:

> '... a bone eure!
> De ce doit il estre molt liez!'
>   (ll.496-97)

and the subject is dropped as abruptly as it was introduced. The only subsequent reference to him is when the lady is seeking to justify taking a lover:

> 'Dont n'ai gë ore esté grant piece
> o mon seignor sanz vilanie?'
>   (ll.698-99)

The remaining characters are the lady's servants and the knight's friends who, after their initial function of encouraging the hero (in lively conversation) to visit the lady, disappear from sight, emerging only to follow the knight unquestioningly on his comings and goings. They are not party to his thoughts (ll.580-82) and do not put any obstacle in his way (ll.712-13). Apart from the brief reference to the husband, then, there is little trace of any character who might constitute an obstacle to a love relationship, the traditional slanderers — opponents of courtly lovers — being barely alluded to in line 8: 'vilains est qui ses gas en fet'. Thus, while it might appear that the protagonists are surrounded by people, these characters are no more clearly defined than the historical or geographical settings of the *Lai*, with the result that nothing can detract from the figures of the knight and the lady.

   The first important stage in the narrative is the presentation of the hero. This is done at considerable length (ll.53-111), but even so the picture that emerges is highly ambiguous. The language draws extensively on the superlatives of courtly love, and abstract nouns figure prominently. Thus the first detail we are given is:

> Proesce et cortoisie l'ot
> eslit a estre suen demainne
>
> (ll.64-65)

and this is soon reinforced by a reference to the knight's moderate speech (l.68) — an indication, perhaps, as to how we are meant to interpret his later conversations? — and his use of material possessions (ll.70-71). Renart then reports on his reputation with women (ll.74-79) and in jousting (ll.82-93). These two aspects of his prowess are not only juxtaposed, but are linguistically associated by the similarity of the lines that conclude each piece of description:

> car il estoit sor toute rien
> et frans et doz et debonnere.
>
> (ll.78-79)

and

> le trovast on [que je ne di]:
> estout et ireus et hardi
>
> (ll.83-84)

and the author seems to be hinting that the adjectives of chivalry (l.84) might equally well be applied to the conquest of women, an idea echoed in line 270. If this is so, it is the first suggestion of the ambiguity in the hero's behaviour that we shall be considering later. The description of the hero then continues with allusions to his love of companionship and games and concludes by comparing the knight favourably to Tristan and reiterating his general courtly qualities (ll.108-11). The last couple of lines constitute the author's judgement on his hero, which is again somewhat sardonic:

> et si estoit plus preuz que beaus,
> et tot ce doit chevaliers estre. (ll.110-11)

Once more the intention does not seem clear cut; in the light of the hero's later development the author may be suggesting that his character's behaviour is to be more prominent than just his fine appearance, and this we shall see is also a source of ambiguity. The different interpretations which can be placed on the hero's actions are prefigured by the early comparison between him and the Arthurian knight Gauvain in line 61. As Cooper (*23*, pp.253-54) has shown, the mention of Gauvain anticipates the possibility of the hero being, similarly, either a playboy or a serious courtly lover.

The section from lines 112 to 211 deals with the one thing lacking in this courtly hero: he has no permanent relationship with a lady, although he has had experience of many (ll.116-19). The presentation of the heroine is thus begun rather obliquely, as the direct effect of Cupid's arrow:

> la grant biauté et le doz non
> d'une dame li mist el cuer.
>
> (ll.130-31)

She is next seen in the hero's imagination:

> ... qui li semble
> li reubiz de toutes biautez.
> Li sens, la debonneretez,
> la grant biauté de son cler vis
> li est, ce li est bien avis,
> devant ses eulz et jor et nuit.
>
> (ll.138-43)

The abstract nouns used again here are once more sufficient for the lady to be regarded as courtly, and the knight's obsession with a lady he has never met constitutes an additional detail of his courtly character. The effect of this is to produce appropriate suffering in the knight and he decides to appeal to the courtly qualities of the lady, which are conveyed in further abstracts: 'gentilesce, pitiez, largece' (l.210). Yet while this seems to be a standard piece of courtly composition, it is rendered ambiguous by the style of the knight's speech. Rather than emphasize his discomfort he imagines instead the women in his past having their revenge and describes the suffering caused by love in comic terms:

> 'c'onques vilains cui barbiers sache
> les denz ne fu si angoisseus!'
> (ll.160-61)

We shall see in a later chapter that this technique is typical of Renart's style, and its effect here is to lead us to question the hero's sincerity. Is he perhaps mocking the whole courtly convention?

When the knight eventually meets the lady the description of her still lacks detail and tends towards abstraction. As in *La Chastelaine de Vergi* the author is more concerned to describe the knight than the lady, whose essential courtliness is taken for granted. Thus lines 301, 304, 324 and 343 refer simply to her *biauté*; otherwise she is described as 'la preuz, la cortoise' (l.315), she has 'bonté' (l.232) and is 'molt cortoise et sage' (l.341), but there is no single complete description of her. Before that, however, the scene of the knight setting out with his friends to the lady's castle has instances of more obvious *double entendre*, in the speech of the knight. In a sense the whole scene is ambiguous, in that the companions understand something different in the outing from the knight's one intention to meet the lady. Once the reader has been made aware of that, every comment by the hero takes on additional meaning, beginning with his exclamation:

> 'Vëez con cis chastiaus siet bien!'
> Il nel disoit pas tant por rien...
> (ll.227-28)

and continuing in

> 'Il n'en est nus dont j'aie envie
> des chastiaus, se de cestui non'
>
> (ll.248-49)

With the even more suggestive reference to taking possession of the castle in lines 252-54, Renart draws our attention to the ambiguity, saying of the companions:

> Il n'entendent pas a son dire
> le sofisme qu'il lor fesoit
>
> (ll.256-57)

Thus the ambiguity inherent in the terminology of courtly love is complemented by ambiguous behaviour and speech on the part of the hero, as well as by narrative comment.

With this element well established early in the poem we are prepared for several interpretations to be possible in the scenes that follow. The knight wastes no time in his suit of the lady, and after a few lines of courtly expression concludes by suggesting that he wishes to be her 'loial ami', although he undoubtedly has much more in mind. This is clearly recognized by the lady who in replying 'par molt biau sens' (l.376) calls him

> 'Si biaus hon de cors et de mains,
> de braz, et de toute autre rien!'
>
> (ll.382-83)

Thus we are introduced to a setting where both characters are liable to act and talk in a way which is distinctly ambiguous. The lady's reply to the knight's declaration (ll.422-47) next reveals the ambiguity of social convention. She claims that the knight has misinterpreted what she sees as her social obligation to receive him, and states this to be a general problem:

> '... il avient assez sovent,
> quant aucune dame vaillant
> fet aucun chevalier semblant
> de cortoisie et d'ennor fere,

> lors cuident tot lor autre afere
> cil soupirant avoir trové!'
>
> (ll.430-35)

It may be that even this riposte is not wholly serious if we bear in mind previous details of her attitude. In greeting the knight she was described as 'cele qui bon joir ait hui' (l.320), while her welcome was a warm one:

> Ele prent par la main, riant,
> le seignor, sel mainne seoir.
>
> (ll.326-27)

and we have already noted the rather flirtatious tone of lines 381-83.

Once the two main characters have been presented and contact between them has been established, with due acknowledgement of the ambiguous nature of social obligations, it is in their subsequent behaviour that ambiguity is now to be observed. The details of their conversations and particular linguistic ambiguities will be discussed in the next two chapters; for the remainder of this chapter we shall be concerned with the different interpretations that may be given to the actions of the characters.

Two possible readings of *Le Lai de l'ombre* have been proposed in an article by Sarah Kay (25) from which a third possibility also emerges. The first suggestion is that the knight at the beginning of the story is ignorant of the nature of true love, and gradually achieves courtliness as the lady's resistance enables him to distinguish true values. According to this reading the knight would genuinely (and ingenuously) take the lady's polite welcome as indicative of deeper feelings, and the acceptance of this point of view would depend on Kay's rather dubious assumption that the knight's lack of experience of true love makes him unable to understand fully the nature of *Amors*. The second suggestion is that the knight is able to hide his passionate feelings behind social convention to the extent that the lady in turn is deceived, until the episode at the well, as to the strength of her own feelings. Put more simply, this seems to amount to a choice between the two aspects of Gauvain reflected in the hero (who, as Kay points out, page 517, prefers in any case to compare himself with Tristan — line 457): is he a philanderer or a genuine courtly lover? Is the *Lai* telling the story of the opportunist's 'conversion' or of a sentimental education of an innocent during which courtliness is achieved? The *double entendre* of passages such as that at lines 227-71 would need to be interpreted either as revealing hidden depths of passion or as simply bawdy asides for the benefit of the knight's companions.

The third possibility which Kay adds almost as an afterthought seems to me to deserve more serious attention. She suggests that neither character is self-deceiving, but that 'both characters are in fact cynically aware of going through the forms of a conventional courtship in order to end up where they both want to be, in each other's arms' (*25*, p.527). Whichever viewpoint is favoured, however, the ambiguity of the romance lies essentially in the contrast between the conventional 'abstract' forms of expression and the underlying reality of the characters' emotions. The fact that the precise nature of those emotions is also obscured by the author increases the range of meanings discernible in certain key episodes in the book.

The attitude of the lady seems to be a little easier to define than that of the knight, thanks to the fleeting insight into her thoughts offered by the short reverie of lines 546-61. Although this is partly a formal device to enable the knight to slip his ring on to her finger unnoticed, it is also the turning point in the romance, with the lady's realization at this stage that:

> ne que jamés si debonnere
> ami n'avra, s'el n'a cestui
>
> (ll.554-55)

We are invited to see the lady as being convinced now of the knight's sincerity:

> El ne le tient mie a faintié
> les soupirs, les lermes qu'il pleure
>
> (ll.550-51)

and herself struggling with *Resons*:

> qu'ele se gart de fere chose
> dont ele se repente au loing.
>
> (ll.560-61)

Yet although this implies potential acceptance of the knight we know nothing of her own feelings. Thus in the second part of the poem we may see the lady either as being obsessed with appearances until the knight's courtly behaviour eventually breaks down the barrier, or as leading him on until she can show herself to be won over, a view perhaps supported by lines 704-05, which insist that the lover must earn her favour. Again either interpretation may be seen as the real working out of the abstract conflict between Love and Reason proposed by courtly tradition.

Action in *Le Lai de l'ombre* is chiefly restricted to the two occasions when the knight gives the lady his ring. The first time it is put on her finger and she rejects his uncourtly act. The second time he throws the ring to her reflection in the well, and this is heralded as an act of supreme courtliness and she accepts him. Both actions are in a sense paradoxical. In the first episode the knight's behaviour is, by any standard, unacceptable and it is surprising to find the hero forcing a love token upon the lady in the context of a narrative so steeped in courtly tradition. In the second, on the other hand, the lady is won by having the love token thrown away (cf. Adler's interpretation, *21*, p.2). Both actions are thus totally contrary to our expectations and are also startling in that their meaning is the opposite to that suggested by appearances.

The circumstances of the uncourtly act also seem to create a setback in the lady's developing feelings as she now views the knight's previous behaviour as false ('faus semblanz', l.596 and 'faus soupirs', l.599) in the light of his abrupt departure. Her reaction at seeing the ring on her finger is open to differing interpretations just as we have seen previous reactions of the protagonists to be. Thus in lines 620-21 she may be admiring the knight's skill in the game in which they are both engaged, or else deploring the advantage he has taken of her. Similarly her emphatic denial that he is her lover (ll.618, 628-29) may be taken to mean 'never' or 'not yet'! The misunderstandings continue when the lady has the knight fetched back. This time the knight is fully aware of the likely reason for the summons (ll.664-67) but prefers not to think about it and concentrate on 'la joie du retor' (l.672): of the two possible interpretations of her calling him back he knowingly selects the less likely but the more pleasurable. The lady's greeting appears to justify the more optimistic interpretation. With the change of scene to the well we have a second structural device which is also significant in the developing romance. The lovers have to move to the well for the final act in the drama, but the knight may also be justified in interpreting the lady's invitation to 'come outside' as a good omen, although its meaning will really prove to be the opposite.

The final part of the *Lai* embodies the conflict between ambiguous appearances and reality which characterizes the whole. It is only the happy ending which is totally free from alternative interpretation. The gesture of throwing the ring to the lady's reflection is undoubtedly *cortoisie* (ll.909, 920), although the process by which the lovers have reached this point is far from clear. Motives, actions and dialogues are all susceptible to different interpretations, leaving us with what Larmat has called 'une œuvre secrète, dont les intentions restent mystérieuses' (*26*, p.414). I have tried to show how the narrative structure of the *Lai* creates such an effect, and in the next chapter I shall be examining Renart's use of dialogue as a further contributive factor.

5. *Le Lai de l'ombre:* The Discourse of Love

The essence of *Le Lai de l'ombre* lies in Renart's art of dialogue, the art which John Stevens terms 'luf-talkyng' (*7*, p.190). On one level this may be admired as a stylistic technique which 'animates the conventional amorous dialogue, transforming it into one of the most elegant and vivacious small masterpieces of medieval fiction' (*28*, p.79). Elegance, however, is only one aspect of Renart's achievement. In purely functional terms the conversations present the necessary conflict between the two protagonists: 'the chivalrous spirit of the Knight clashes with the conventionality of the Lady and makes the dramatic conflict of the Lay' (*22*, p.72), although to this must be added the complicating factor of ambiguity examined in the previous chapter. Yet however admirable in their artistry in style and character portrayal, it is remarkable that in the end these dialogues are not directly effective. We witness the phenomenon of language breaking down under the weight of its own ambiguity. The climax and meaning of the *Lai* are to be found in the paradoxical, but ultimately unambiguous, gesture that replaces and transcends speech. It is perhaps with the advantage of hindsight that Larmat thus reduces the importance of conversation to 'servant de commentaire au mimodrame' (*26*, p.441). However it is the dialogues that prepare us for and make possible this dénouement, and in this chapter I should like to examine the distribution, function and nature of those dialogues.

It is perhaps significant that the beginning of the encounter between the lady and the knight depends more on the reporting of gesture than on speech, as does the outcome of the story. Apart from the lady's two lines of conversational welcome (ll.318-19) we can judge the actual meeting only through the characters' actions (especially in ll.326-49) and this establishes early in the narrative the question of whether we are being presented with a demonstration of social convention or something

deeper. The knight's declaration of love in lines 350-67 appears
to us abrupt and unexpected only because it occurs in the very
first conversational passage. The characters' courtliness and,
significantly, their equality in the art of conversation have
already been established:

> mes la gentil, la debonnere,
> li set bien rendre par parole
> reson de qanqu'il l'aparole ...
>   (ll.338-40)

Thus we should not be shocked at the knight's sudden
declaration nor consider the lady to be put at any disadvantage.

This first speech relies on the conventions of courtly dialogue
and is not marked by the wordplay and shifts in tone which
characterize some of the subsequent exchanges. The knight
begins with a traditional form of address, 'Bele tresdouce amie
chiere' (l.350) and ends with his desire to be her 'loial ami'
(l.367). It contains a rhetorical use of synonyms ('force et pooir'
— l.355), and an unexceptional comparison between the lover as
suppliant and a prayer in church (ll.364-65), together with some
stock terms of courtly vocabulary (*joie, merci, gentillece, pitiez*).
The lady's reply, in contrast, already appears more vivacious,
and the author prejudges it as having 'molt biau sens' (l.376). It
appears more spontaneous (note the effect of the break in line
379) and contains only one reference to courtly tradition — the
idea of the lover achieving merit through his love, a motif that
recurs near the end of the poem. Instead we have the slightly
flirtatious reference to the knight's physical attributes already
noted (ll.382-83) and the use of a colloquialism (ll.384-86) which
perhaps serves to lighten her rejection.

The suggestion that the lady has the advantage over her suitor
is echoed in the narrator's comment that the knight dared not
contradict her (l.397), and when the dialogue resumes it follows
a pattern similar to that of the first two exchanges. Again the
knight falls back on courtliness for his argument, pleading that
he will indeed prove himself worthy of her, while the lady's reply
is more dramatic and varied. She supports her view that the

knight has acted *folement* (l.427) with a general picture of uncourtly behaviour (ll.429-35) and follows it with another lively comparison:

> 'Miex vos venist avoir tendu
> la hors une roiz a colons!'
> (ll.438-39)

before refuting the knight's argument about acquiring valour from courting her. The fact that there is little or no authorial comment to separate such exchanges helps create an impression of lively argument, which is developed further in part two when the knight begins to match the lady's spirit with his own.

It is towards the end of part one that we begin to see the limitations of dialogue. There are first of all breaks in the conversation as Renart pauses to describe the physical effect of the dialogue on the knight, which in turn begins to convince the lady of his good faith. As Payen notes, 'le véritable amour ne s'accomplit que dans la communication silencieuse, lorsqu'enfin l'être se révèle par d'autres voies que la parole' (5, p.185). At this stage, of course, the visible demonstration of love is one-sided, as the author is quick to point out:

> Certes, s'ele plorast avec,
> la dame molt fesist grant bien
> (ll.488-89)

Then, secondly, the knight, who has begun to win the lady over by his appearance where words have failed, finally gains his temporary advantage not by speech but by a gesture. Thus lines 512-44 are concerned with the knight's request to the lady to accept a love token and her refusal of it, and in the ensuing silence the knight is able to slip the ring on her finger. Already we witness the failure of language, for a gesture is needed — albeit an uncourtly one — for the dialogue to be re-established and for the process of courtship to be continued.

By this stage too in the story a note of self-consciousness seems to have become apparent in the voice both of the narrator

and of his characters. Thus Renart tends to open his subsections
by alluding to the negative effects of the hero's words (cf. ll.388-
89, 448-49, 476-77), while the lady's silence is induced by 'cil
biau mot plesant et poli' (l.546). We have already noted the
author's allusion to the lady's verbal skills (ll.338-40) and these
are explicitly combatted by the knight, e.g.:

> 'Molt mal s'i acorde et asent
> vostre parole a vos biax eulz,
> qui m'acueillirent orainz mielz
> au venir, et plus pesamment.'
>
> (ll.402-05)

or in reply to her refusals,

> 'Gardez, nu fetes mes por rien'
>
> (l.513)

The lady's monologue which opens the second part sets the
tone for the remaining dialogue by virtue of its spontaneity. In
particular the short exclamations and rhetorical questions that
follow the lady's discovery of the ring on her finger anticipate
the scene where she tries to persuade the knight to take it back
(cf. ll.795-805). Her confusion and recourse to various forms of
optatives and commands (ll.631-41) also reflect the change in
balance of the situation with its movement towards the knight's
advantage. Her closing monologue before the knight returns
again makes explicit her concern for language (ll.689, 691, 703);
it is only when confronted by non-verbal communication — the
knight's tears, his actions with the ring — that she is at a loss.

The lady's greeting of the knight on his return reveals the
ambiguity which characterizes so much of the dialogue and
might also be assumed to have been present in the unreported
welcome given to the knight at his first entrance. Thus the
knight, whose confident salutation (ll.713-14) goes un-
challenged, is misled into assuming the lady has capitulated
(ll.724-25). The author's indication of a favourable outcome —
the use of *encor* in line 726 is crucial — tends to undermine the

force of the lady's attack. It is, however, just that, for she opens immediately (before he can sit down) with a question inviting the knight to explain his action. This he does with a curious mixture of courtly and uncourtly sentiment. His courtly comment about the increased value of his ring now she has worn it is followed at once with the unseemly wish that everyone should know of their relationship:

> 'S'il vos plesoit, en cest esté
> le savroient mi anemi,
> se vos m'avïez a ami
> reçut, et je vos a amie.'
>
> (ll. 740-43)

This passage may be seen as a further example of the ambiguous intentions of the knight. It may be regarded as the arrogant speech of an experienced lover, the reckless comment of the inexperienced one, or the realistic assessment of a character seeing through the façade of social convention. Whatever the interpretation, however, the lady's spirited rejection leaves the knight in despair.

This is not, however, the end of the matter, for the courtly character in the knight is confronted with the problem of how to take back the ring, and concern for his reputation and other courtly concepts come once more to the fore. But, in contrast to the earlier conversation, the knight's emotion begins to creep in alongside conventional expression:

> 'Diex!' fet il, 'se ge me feroie
> d'un coutel tres par mi la cuisse,
> ne me feroie tele angoisse
> conme ces paroles me font.'
>
> (ll. 772-75)

I have drawn attention elsewhere to the significance of a wound in the thigh (*I*, p.22), with its sexual overtones. It is not infrequently suffered by heroes in romance, but I know of no example where there is the threat of its being self-inflicted. The knight is thus suggesting that the suffering caused by the lady's *words* in refusing his ring is greater than physical pain and, possibly, sexual deprivation. The lady's answer, however, adheres to courtly propriety, as she reminds the knight of his duty: 'Il le vos covient a reprendre' (1.794).

The final stage in the purely verbal conflict is marked by the discarding of courtly language and style in favour of spontaneous emotional argument. This is reflected in the short exchanges of lines 795-803, which recall the syntax of the lady's monologue earlier and also look forward to the brief dialogue which precedes the last scene (ll.888-93). The vocabulary is free from courtly mannerisms, and the passage is a good illustration of the way in which Renart varies his poetic style to suit the emotional demands of the occasion. The lady rebuffs the knight with word play (ll.810-12), while the knight answers her with colloquialisms (ll.814ff.). Nevertheless, the lady has to conclude that language is powerless (ll.822-23) and her final argument is an appeal to his courtly good faith:

> 'par la grant foi que me devez
> et proier que le reprenez
> si chier con vos avez m'amor.'
> (ll.825-27)

This marks the end of the dialogue of any significance in the poem. The knight has apparently failed to move the lady by argument, whether or not this is couched in courtly terms, and contact has been maintained thus far thanks only to an uncourtly gesture. Similarly, the lady's skill with words has proved insufficient in the face of the knight's obstinacy, and she has to fall back on social convention for her final argument.

The courtly action which constitutes the poem's dénouement is mainly prepared not by dialogue but by a monologue in which the genuine nature of the knight's intention is now clear. The brief conversation before the ring is thrown into the well, however, continues to reflect the ambiguity of the whole relationship so far. Thus the lady is mistakenly led to interpret the knight's behaviour as being about to return the ring to his own finger, following his understated compliment:

> 'por ce n'est pas li ors nerciz',
> fet il, 's'il vient de vo biau doit!'
> (ll.872-73 and cf. earlier ll.738-39)

The lady's swift reaction to the knight's intention may be seen as sudden jealousy, while the knight's final comment on his action, 'Molt en est amendez mes pris' (l.902), answers his own arguments earlier. But these short speeches are little more than glosses on the action, which has become central. Indeed, once the ring has been thrown into the well, little else needs to be said. Just as the action was introduced by the knight's monologue, which replaces conversation, so it is followed by the lady's unspoken reaction. Her verbal acceptance of the knight is one of extreme simplicity. Yet, although we have seen how ambiguous language gives way to gesture, the lady's final speech suggests that both are necessary:

> 'tot vostre cuer ont el mien mis
> cil doz mot et cil plesant fet,
> et li dons que vos avez fet
> a mon ombre, en l'onor de moi ...'
> (ll.932-35)

Language has perhaps been reinstated since it has, after all, been shown to be based on good faith; only in retrospect, however, may the dialogues be seen as examples of *doz mot*.

By looking at the occurrence of dialogue throughout the poem we obviously gain some idea of its function. The alternative views of the knight as dallying or passionate find some support in the details of the conversations, as does the possibility that both the lady and the knight are merely indulging in the ritual demanded by propriety. Yet this, even when taken in conjunction with the ambiguous behaviour and attitudes of the protagonists, does not offer a complete explanation for the breakdown of language and its replacement by gesture. We need to consider more closely the links between their speeches to establish the extent to which the characters are actually able to communicate with each other by purely linguistic means.

The first dialogue in part one is a good example both of the way in which Renart's characters interact and also of how he demonstrates the limitations of language. The knight's declaration to the lady is made in superlatives: 'il n'est rien nule que j'ain tant / conme vos' (ll.357-58) and 'Vos toute seule avez pooir / sor moi, plus que dame qui vive' (ll.372-73) and the lady's answer, similarly, is couched in as near superlative terms as decorum permits:

> '... je ne croi mie
> que si biaus hon soit sanz amie
> con vos estes; nus nu creroit.
> Vostre pris en abesseroit,
> et si en vauriez molt mains ...'
>
> (ll.377-81)

Two processes are at work here. Firstly the lady is indirectly revealing the impression that the knight has made on her ('si biaus hon'), and secondly, having rejected the knight's plea that she is his only beloved, she is introducing the line of argument that he must answer, the idea of loss of *pris*. The knight's reply contains similar elements. He begins by answering her impression with his own reference to her 'biax eulz' (l.403) while suggesting that her looks belie her words. He then answers the argument she has presented with the courtly idea that his valour will increase through her. The lady's reply, however, seems to be meant to show that her interpretation of courtliness is not his. When she has defended her courteous welcome of him, all the points raised have been answered, and the knight, defeated, falls silent:

> Or ne set cil, n'en dit n'en fait,
> qu'il puist fere ne devenir
>
> (ll.448-49)

His final speech in this section is no more than a plea for mercy, and the narrator emphasizes his defeat:

> Que qu'il puist dire ne prometre,
> a ce ne li puet rien valoir
>
> (ll.476-77)

Much more effective, however, is non-verbal communication — the emotion revealed in his face — and this leads the lady to initiate the second stage of their conversation.

From line 492 the dialogue follows a similar pattern, with each speaker answering the point made by the other. When a point is left uncontested the exchanges falter, and as a result the lady turns to soliloquy, and speech is replaced by gesture. The lady's new line of attack, that she has a duty towards her husband, is countered by the knight in words which again reveal his high opinion of himself: in courtly terms she would acquire honour through taking him as a lover (l.502), an honour comparable to the merit of undertaking a pilgrimage (ll.504-05)! The connotations of the latter are at once picked up by the lady who tells the knight that he should go (*partir*, l.506) and that his request is *oiseuse proiere* (l.510).

At the end of the first part it is the knight who begins a new line of argument, with his request that she should accept a love token. This idea is rejected by the lady:

> 'Sire, je ne veil pas avoir',
> fet la dame, 'le lox sans preu'
>
> (ll.526-27)

Hers is another courtly argument, but she does not appear to react to the courtly approach used by the knight both before and after this rejection. His speech offering a token begins 'Ha! dame, ... mort m'avez!', and this is developed in his reply:

> 'Se vos me lessïez morir
> sanz estre amez, ce seroit teche,
> se cil biaus vis plains de simplece
> estoit omecide de moi'
>
> (ll.538-41)

It is possible that it is the picture of a dying lover which finally reduces the lady to silence and prepares the way for the second part of the poem:

> Cil biau mot plesant et poli
> le font en un pensé chaïr
>
> (ll.546-47)

Whether or not this is so, the pattern of the dialogue in the poem thus far has shown each protagonist taking up and refuting the arguments put forward by the other. Where a point is unanswerable, first the knight and then the lady become silent, and emotions are communicated through that silence, as well as through the tears of the knight.

In part two there seems to be much more frequent use of courtly terminology. It is interesting that although the characters may try to conceal their feelings in such conventional expression, this tends to happen only after we have been given a very good idea as to what those feelings are. We have seen already how the dialogue towards the end of the poem becomes more heated, and the exchanges more rapid, but Renart's technique remains the same, with the characters taking up each other's points, albeit in a more urgent way.

The knight's reply to the lady's opening gambit:

> 'c'est vostre anel que je tien ci —
> por qoi le me donnastes ore?'
>
> (ll.732-33)

is unfortunate (ll.734ff.), and, as we have seen, uncourtly, undermining his courtly plea that the ring's value is increased through being on her finger. His idea that everyone should know of his love ('le savroient mi anemi' — l.741) is at once rebuked in similar terms by the lady: 'vos avroiz ne cri ne non / de m'amor ...' (ll.748-49) and stressed by her colloquial reminder: 'Vos n'en estes pas en la voie' (l.750). As the narrator tells us (ll.756-57), the knight is in despair, and this is expressed in a lament for his courtly *pris* (l.758) and lack of *joie* (l.760). The lady's tone (noticeably altered from that used in her previous speech) at once changes to fit his, and she replies with a courtly argument to the effect that she is not to blame: 'Je ne faz mie grant outrage ...' (l.766). In his reply to this the knight first confesses his anguish in straightforward terms before returning to conventional ideas, this time the cliché of leaving his heart with the ring in her service. When the lady insists — and in lines 789-93 she is reminiscent of the haughty *dompna* of Provençal origin with a commanding *volenté* — the thinly-veiled basic emotions break through: '"[Non] fet!" "[Si] fet!"' (l.795) and this happens again a few lines later (ll.801-03). At this point the logical thread which has run through the dialogue so far is lost, and ll.810-19 are little more than an exchange of insults. The argument ends with the lady's final appeal to the knight 'par la grant foi que me devez' (l.825).

As the conversation draws to a close, the author reports the knight's dilemma (ll.829-31) and then has him state it with reference to a literary genre, the *jeu parti* (ll.832ff.) — a stylized debate; in this Renart is following the same procedure as before, using literary convention to express a real situation. The conclusion of the knight's monologue is an acceptance of the lady's wishes, again presented in courtly terms (ll.854-57). This return to courtly expression may also be seen as preparation for the action that is to follow. Similarly, when the knight has thrown the ring into the well, he recognizes the courtly merit of what he has done (l.902), although this is followed by a franker comment on the lack of barriers between himself and the reflection. Once the discordant note in the dialogue has disappeared, therefore, courtly expression returns, as the lady in turn recognizes the value of the knight's action (ll.918-20). The final exchange between the couple hinges on the idea of *onor* (ll.935, 940) but is characterized by linguistic simplicity, as the need for purely verbal communication is removed.

Both parts of the *Lai de l'ombre*, therefore, demonstrate the collapse of dialogue, but for slightly different reasons. At the end of part one silence is imposed because of the ambiguity of the situation. The lady cannot give in because, as Payen puts it, 'le langage galant est impuissant à la persuader, parce que ce langage est trop souvent celui de la mauvaise foi' (*5*, p.186). In part two, the language of the dialogue still conveys both genuine feeling and stylized emotions, and comes to an abrupt halt first when the former takes precedence in a slanging match. Silence falls at the end because the situation is no longer ambiguous and has no need of deceptive linguistic expression. Gesture has become the prime means of communication because it is an 'interprète plus sûr des sentiments profonds' (*26*, p.411). The discourse of love in *Le Lai de l'ombre* is not then to be equated simply with dialogue. Its meaning is compounded in part out of language with all its ambiguities, but also out of the gradual effacing of reasoned argument and out of the gestures that complement, and ultimately take precedence over, language.

6. *Le Lai de l'ombre:* Renart's Style

We have seen in chapter 4 how ambiguity seems to be built into the narrative structure of *Le Lai de l'ombre*, both in the conflicting interpretations which may be given to the characters' speech and behaviour and also in the protagonists' relationship with each other — what Sarah Kay calls 'a curious balance of opposition and sympathy' (*25*, p.525). In the last chapter we saw how this is reflected in language, with the result that gesture (itself not free from ambiguity) ultimately replaces speech as a means of communication. The question that remains is how the style of *Le Lai de l'ombre* helps create these different strands of meaning. Particularly characteristic of the work is a divergence between form and content, for example courtly language describing a possibly uncourtly character, or colloquial expressions used at moments of dramatic tension. This results in a certain distance between the author and his work, with the result that the author's attitude towards his characters is rarely wholly clear.

Critics vary in the extent to which they are prepared to claim stylistic deviation from the norm on the part of Renart. Thus Lejeune-Dehousse sees his originality in terms of verbal incisiveness: 'Les œuvres de Jean Renart, qui comptent très peu de clichés chers à la littérature courtoise, se distinguaient par leur emploi du mot juste, de l'expression incisive' (*27*, p.297). Beekman proposes, more generally, a personal style achieved in much the same way as that of the author of *La Chastelaine de Vergi*: 'With the thirteenth-century literary tradition as a base, [the writings of Jean Renart] rise through modifications, adaptations and changes to a personal form created by their author' (*22*, p.62). Larmat, however, suggests that the divergence is more extreme: 'L'œuvre garde tellement ses distances par rapport aux conventions de l'amour courtois que tous les traits qui lui appartiennent ne sont peut-être là que pour en faire la satire' (*26*, p.408). What I shall try to show in the next few pages is that the style of *Le Lai de l'ombre* should not be described as a modification of the *style courtois* so much as a juxtaposing of courtly elements and of features from other registers. The result is a style which fosters ambiguity and thus contributes significantly to the meaning of the poem as a whole. This will, I hope, be clear if we consider in turn the poem's main stylistic components.

Firstly, the formal features of the poem. I have already mentioned several critics who have tried to establish a more complex formal origin for *Le Lai de l'ombre* than that of the *lai* (p.56 above), and this preoccupation is perhaps also reflected elsewhere in an emphasis on Renart's versification. In an early study of the *Lai* (and one typical of the scholarship of the time) Färber commented on an unusually high number of *enjambements* and 'rich rhymes' in the poem, but without offering any explanation for it (*24*, p.700ff.). Beekman (*22*, Introduction) notes the recurrent pattern of a 3 + 5 division of the eight-syllable line; he also lists three types of end rhyme, suggesting (significantly for my view of ambiguity as being of the essence) that the rhyming of different meanings of the same word is the most frequent type. These points are summed up in Sweetser's comment on Renart's free use of the couplet in *L'Escoufle*: 'Le poète, gêné par les contraintes imposées par une métrique rigoureuse, semble vouloir rompre non seulement la rigidité des couplets, mais manier la langue d'une façon si libre et désinvolte que le sens risque de ne plus apparaître clairement' (*29*, p.xxxviii). The significance of Renart's innovatory tendencies in this respect soon becomes clear when we look at some of the contexts of, particularly, homonymous rhymes and of this more flexible treatment of the couplet.

I have already drawn attention to Renart's habit of making the rhyming couplet cut across the semantic structure of the lines, which helps to create a flowing and apparently unbroken narrative. This effect is emphasized when the rhymes in question are homonymous. Thus the comparison between the knight and Tristan is stressed in that properties of each are linked:

si li fist en tens et en lieu
sentir son pooir et sa *force*:
c'onques Tristans, qui fu a *force*
tonduz conme fox por Yseut
(ll.122-25; my italics)

The knight and the lady are associated in the same way:

La colors l'en croit et avive
de ce qu'il dit qu'il est toz *sens*.
Puis li a dit par molt biau *sens* ...
(ll.374-76; my italics)

Similarly, when the lady has sent her messenger after the knight,
the rhyme links the characters and contributes to the narrative
movement:

Ce li fist son oirre amender,
qu'il tarde cele qu'el le *voie*.
Li escuiers s'est en la *voie*
du retor a lui acointiez.
(ll.660-63; my italics)

The same rhyme is used earlier in the poem when the knight
pretends to allow himself to be persuaded by his friends to visit
the lady:

font cil, 'Chevaliers ne doit onques
trespasser n'e[n] chemin n'en voie
bele dame, qu'il ne la voie.'
(ll.262-64)

At other points too in the poem homonymic rhymes have a
special emphatic function as, for example, when the crucial
element of the well is introduced unwittingly by the lady:

'... Se je puis,
ainz le menré desor ce puis;

> si parlerai illec a lui.'
>
> (ll.687-89)

The same feature occurs in the knight's exclamation after he has thrown the ring into the well:

> 'Vez, dame!' fet il, 'or l'a pris.
> Molt en est amendez mes pris,
> quant ce, qui de vos est, l'enporte.'
>
> (ll.901-03)

The other striking aspect of Renart's versification is his use of broken lines. This is particularly effective in the dialogue sections, where realistic, emotional speech is suggested. The same device enables these sections to stand out from the narrative, as Renart regularly inserts *fet il*, *fet ele*, and so on at the beginning of a speech. At moments of crisis, however, we find not one but two breaks in the line, for example in the lady's monologue when she has discovered the ring on her finger:

> 'De tant sui je bien en mon sens
> que je vi orainz en son doit
> cestui; ce fis mon, orendroit.'
>
> (ll.614-16)

and a number of other broken lines follow this. The argument between the knight and the lady is given urgency in the same way:

> '[Non] fet!' '[Si] fet! la n'a que dire'
>
> (l.795)

and there are a number of examples in the exchanges that follow. Renart's versification, then, helps to create the poem's unity and forms part of its distinctive style; it is flexible enough to assist the emergence of a distinctive form of dialogue and to emphasize relationships and turning points in the poem.

I should like now to consider briefly the vocabulary of the

poem and the different areas of language from which it is drawn, since it is this variety and the juxtaposition of terms from different fields which prevent the poem from having one consistent tone. At the outset, however, the dominant impression is of a courtly love setting, as the conventional courtly adjectives and abstract nouns are used to present first the knight and then the lady (cf. pp.61-63 above). But there are already several ways in which the poem's vocabulary is broadened beyond this. In the description of the knight the language of chivalry is added to courtliness:

> le trovast on [que je ne di]:
> estout et ireus et hardi
> quant il avoit l'eaume en son chief.
> (ll.83-85)

This then leads on to a further linguistic peculiarity, the unexpected use of colloquialisms or popular sayings. Of the knight it is said that his chivalrous enthusiasm was such that

> ... il vosist que chascun lundi
> qu[ë] il estoit qu'il en fust deus!
> (ll.90-91)

(For a discussion of the significance of Monday here, a day for tournaments, see *30*.) The combination of the chivalrous and the popular is reflected further in the young men's 'battle cry' as they set out: 'As armes, chevalier!' (l.270). After this the chivalrous nuances are dropped, although there is an echo of them perhaps in the implicit comparison between the knight and a docile horse: 'Il se sueffre a mener tendant' (l.392).

A further feature drawn from courtly style is the allegorical reference to *Amors*. This occurs frequently near the beginning of the poem (ll.112, 128, 147, 165), and then is used only in the crucial episodes at the end of part one and beginning of part two, and once again at the end of the poem. In these last instances another personified abstract appears: in her soliloquy the lady is beset by the conflicting claims of *Resons* and *Amors* (ll.559 and 566), while the epilogue refers to *sens et Amors* (l.956). Thus Renart does not dominate his work with certain lexical items, but having established courtly terms at the outset he then uses them more sparingly in the course of the poem, to good effect. Other areas of vocabulary are drawn on for isolated stylistic effects, for instance the use of legal terminology in line 464:

> 'Un tel plet m'a mes cuers basti
> quë en vos s'est mis sanz congié'
>   (ll.464-65)

or the possible feudal overtones in lines 522-23:

> 'Vo douz vis et vo clere face
> me puent de pou ostagier'

The most striking aspect of Renart's language, however, is the inclusion of colloquialisms and proverbs or popular sayings, at unexpected moments in the poem. This is the most obvious way in which there is discrepancy between form and content, contributing to the ambiguous tone of the whole. It is to be found in passages concerned with the speech or thoughts of both knight and lady, and in addition in the author's prologue and epilogue. The first colloquialism occurs as early as lines 16-17. Then lines 45-48 contain a pun on the theme of poetic composition, and another on similar lines is used to close the poem (l.962).

The suspicion that Renart may be making fun of literary art, which is often the subject of serious and obscure digressions in longer poems (cf. Marie de France's prologue to her *Lais*), is echoed by the knight's use of 'catch phrases' in his deliberations on whether to court the lady. He seems to be debunking the ideal of courtly suffering in the following:

> 'lors quier par mon lit et atast
> son biau cors qui m'art et esprant.
> Mes, las! "qui ne trueve ne prent"'!

> C'est avenu moi et maint autre
> mainte foiz...'
>
> (ll.182-86)

and his use of a proverb to convey his decision to see her (ll.202-03) may also imply a certain lack of authenticity. After that, however, it is in the speech of the lady that spirited colloquialisms occur (e.g. ll.385-86, 438-39, 687). Only in part two, where, as we have already noted, the knight becomes more adventurous in his language, does he counter the lady's arguments in this way (ll.716-17, 815). In these instances, however, I feel that Renart is varying the linguistic tone to make his characters' conversation more lively and realistic, thereby exposing the inadequacies of conventional courtly dialogue.

The use of colloquialisms throughout *Le Lai de l'ombre* is all the more notable since Renart makes extensive use of rhetorical figures, which contribute further to the poem's stylistic variety. The most frequent feature is pairs of synonyms. These are sometimes clichés of courtly language, e.g.:

> '...qu'ele m'estraint et embrace' (l.179)

> Il fu soupiranz et pensis (l.584)

and sometimes involve less predictable terms:

> '... me fet gerpir et geter puer' (l.352)

> 'Mal fet qui destruit et confont ...' (l.776)

A less frequent rhetorical figure in the *Lai* is litotes, which is generally applied to the behaviour of the lovers, and occasionally used by them in paying a courtly compliment. Thus we are given the lady's reaction to the knight's first entrance:

> N'en devint pas vermeille d'ire
> la dame, ainz en ot grant merveille
> (ll.296-97)

and later her feelings for him after their conversation:

> El ne le tient mie a faintié
> les soupirs, les lermes qu'il pleure
> (ll.550-51)

Both characters use understatement in speaking of their rings as
love tokens; firstly there is the knight's description of his own:

> 'Por ce n'est pas li ors nerciz',
> fet il, 's'il vient de vo biau doit.'
> (ll.872-73)

and secondly the lady's gift of hers to him:

> 'Je cuit que vos ne l'avrez mie
> mains du vostre, encor soit il pire.'
> (ll.938-39)

Although litotes is a fairly familiar feature of courtly writing, its
occurrence is significant here in that it involves linguistic
ambiguity — what is said is not exactly what is meant.

Other rhetorical figures occur sporadically in the course of the
poem (see, for example, the *annominatio* in lines 216-23), but
never to the extent of imposing a dominant rhetorical flavour.
Instead the combination of elevated and popular levels of
language, together with the lively tone of the dialogues, creates
an original stylistic pattern, which gives rise to humorous and
ironic effects, as well as forming an integral part of the poem's
ambiguity.

Conclusion

I began by noting a few features common to both *La Chastelaine de Vergi* and *Le Lai de l'ombre*, and I should like to end by stressing some of the differences in direction followed by these two romances. The preceding chapters have shown the tenets of courtly love to be the point of departure of both texts, with each developing its own way of putting the abstract ideals into practice. The author of *La Chastelaine de Vergi* chooses to dramatize the key theme of secrecy and to place the emphasis on a series of actions resulting from an initial betrayal. Jean Renart in *Le Lai de l'ombre*, however, does not seek action beyond the scope of gesture. Instead the conventions and language of courtly love are questioned, and this questioning is the focal point of the whole poem. Both authors make use intermittently of the linguistic clichés of courtly love; in *La Chastelaine de Vergi* these are combined with simple, 'sober' language to produce a concise and fast-moving narrative, whereas in *Le Lai de l'ombre* they contribute to a style which intermingles linguistic tones and which is paralleled by a narrative where several different interpretations are possible.

In form we have seen that both romances are carefully structured, with *La Chastelaine de Vergi* exhibiting a greater complexity, which reflects the elaborate development of the theme of revelation. Thus it stands in the tradition of the courtly narrative, while *Le Lai de l'ombre*, through its emphasis on language, has much in common with the courtly lyric. Thematically it might be argued that both works have their origin in the courtly virtue of discretion. In *La Chastelaine de Vergi* this is equated with fidelity, while in *Le Lai de l'ombre* it is examined in forms of courtship; in the former the ideal proves to be impossible, while in the latter it succeeds only through the ingenuity of the hero, when traditional arguments have failed him. Both works, too, are concerned with identity. *La*

Chastelaine de Vergi shows the progressive revelation of the identity of the chastelaine's lover; *Le Lai de l'ombre*, however, centres on a more subtle investigation — that of the lover's inner identity, the authenticity, or otherwise, of his emotions.

Finally, I come back to Stevens's suggestion (quoted p.11 above) that there must be a certain universality inherent in the medieval love-romance. Linguistically, this is reflected in the near or total anonymity of the characters in both works. Thematically, the argument in *La Chastelaine de Vergi* that society cannot tolerate secret love undermining its structure is one that is clearly timeless. *Le Lai de l'ombre* is perhaps less obviously universal in its message, in that it seems more intimately dependent on the conventions of a particular age and society. If, however, we view it as concerned with exposing the ritualistic nature of courtship and the conflict between institutionalised language and human emotion, then the poem's import at once transcends its thirteenth-century setting. Both romances, then, while exemplifying different strands of a common tradition, may be seen together as inspired products of the medieval poets' fascination with the timeless complexities of courtship and love.

Select Bibliography

GENERAL

1. Clifford, P.M., *Marie de France: 'Lais'* (London: Grant and Cutler, 1982).
2. Dubuis, R., *Les 'Cent nouvelles nouvelles' et la tradition de la nouvelle en France au moyen âge* (Grenoble: Presses Universitaires, 1973).
3. Fox, J., *A Literary History of France in the Middle Ages* (London and New York: Ernest Benn, 1974).
4. Lefay-Toury, M.-N., *La Tentation du suicide dans le roman du XIIe siècle* (Paris: Champion, 1979).
5. Payen, J.-C., 'Structure et sens de *Guillaume de Dôle*' (1973) reprinted in *Der altfranzösische höfische Roman*, ed. E. Köhler (Darmstadt: Wissenschaftliche Buchgesellschaft, 1978), 170-88.
6. Rossman, V.L., *Perspectives of Irony in Medieval French Literature* (Paris-The Hague: Mouton, 1975).
7. Stevens, J., *Medieval Romance: themes and approaches* (London: Hutchinson, 1973).
8. Voretsch, K., *Introduction to the Study of Old French Literature* (Halle: Niemeyer, 1931).
9. Zumthor, P., *Histoire littéraire de la France médiévale, VIe-XIVe siècles* (Paris: PUF, 1954).

LA CHASTELAINE DE VERGI

10. Arrathoon, L.A., '*The Châtelaine de Vergi*: a structural study of an old French artistic short narrative', *Language and Style*, 7 (1974), 151-80.
11. Frappier, J., '*La Chastelaine de Vergi*, Marguerite de Navarre et Bandello', *Publications de la Faculté des Lettres de l'Université de Strasbourg: Mélanges 1945*, II: *Etudes littéraires* (Paris: Les Belles Lettres, 1946), 89-150.
12. Kostoroski, E.P., 'Quest in query and the *Chastelaine de Vergi*', *Medievalia et Humanistica* 3 (1972), 179-98.
13. Lakits, P., '*La Chastelaine de Vergi*' et l'évolution de la nouvelle courtoise*, Studia Romanica, Universitatis Debreceniensis de Ludovico Kossuth nominatae, 11 (Debrecen, 1966).
14. Maraud, A., 'Le Lai de *Lanval* et *La Chastelaine de Vergi*: la structure narrative', *Romania*, 93 (1972), 433-59.
15. Payen, J.-C., 'Structure et sens de *La Chastelaine de Vergi*', *Le Moyen Age*, 79 (1973), 209-30.

16. Reed, J., '*La Chastelaine de Vergi*: was the heroine married?', *Romance Notes*, 16 (1974), 197-204.

17. Rychner, J., 'La présence et le point de vue du narrateur dans deux récits courts: *Le Lai de Lanval* et *La Chastelaine de Vergi*', *Vox Romanica*, 39 (1980), 86-103.

18. Shirt, D.J., '*La Chastelaine de Vergi*: the technique of stylistic cohesion', *Reading Medieval Studies*, 6 (1980), 81-99.

19. Stuip, R.E.V., '*La Chastelaine de Vergi*'. *Edition critique du B.N.f.fr.375 ... suivie de l'édition diplomatique de tous les manuscrits connus du XIIIe et du XIVe siècle* (Paris-The Hague: Mouton, 1970).

20. Zumthor, P., 'De la chanson au récit: *La Chastelaine de Vergi*' (1968), reprinted in *Der altfranzösische höfische Roman* (Darmstadt: Wissenschaftliche Buchgesellschaft, 1978), 229-53.

LE LAI DE L'OMBRE

21. Adler, A., 'Rapprochement et éloignement comme thèmes du *Lai de l'ombre*', *Etudes de philologie romane et d'histoire littéraire offertes à J. Horrent* (Liege: 1980), 1-4.

22. Beekman, P.H., *Jean Renart and his writings* (Paris: Droz, 1935).

23. Cooper, L.F., 'The literary reflectiveness of Jean Renart's *Lai de l'ombre*', *Romance Philology*, 35 (1981), 250-60.

24. Färber, E., 'Die Sprache der dem Jean Renart zugeschriebenen Werke *Lai de l'ombre, Roman de la Rose ou de Guillaume de Dôle* und *Escoufle*', *Romanische Forschungen*, 33 (1913), 683-793.

25. Kay, S., 'Two readings of the *Lai de l'ombre*', *Modern Language Review*, 75 (1980), 515-27.

26. Larmat, J., 'La morale de Jean Renart dans *Le Lai de l'ombre*', *Mélanges de philologie romane offerts à Charles Camproux*, I (Montpellier: C.E.O., 1978).

27. Lejeune-Dehousse, R., *L'Œuvre de Jean Renart: contribution à l'étude du genre romanesque au moyen âge* (Paris: Droz, 1935).

28. Sargent, B.N., 'The *Lai de l'ombre* and the *De Amore*', *Romance Notes*, 7 (1965), 73-79.

29. Sweetser, F. (ed.), *Jean Renart: 'L'Escoufle', roman d'aventure* (Paris and Geneva: Droz, 1974).

30. Vigneras, L., 'Monday as a date for medieval tournaments, I: A propos du *Lai de l'ombre*', *Modern Language Notes*, 48 (1933), 80-82.

31. ——, 'Etudes sur Jean Renart, II: Sur la date du *Lai de l'ombre*', *Modern Philology*, 30 (1933), 351-59.

CRITICAL GUIDES TO FRENCH TEXTS

edited by

Roger Little, Wolfgang van Emden, David Williams